DO YOU REALLY TRUST THE LORD?

Steven Thorpe

DO YOU REALLY TRUST THE LORD?

Kingdom Publishers

Copyright© Steven Thorpe 2025

All rights reserved. No part of this book may be reproduced in any form by photocopying or any electronic or mechanical means, including information storage or retrieval systems, without permission in writing from both the copyright owner and the publisher of the book. The right of Steven Thorpe to be identified as the author of this work has been asserted by him in accordance with the Copyright, Designs, and Patents Act 1988 and any subsequent amendments thereto.

A catalogue record for this book is available from the British Library.

All Scripture quotations have been taken from the King James version of the Bible

ISBN: 978-1-916801-30-1

1st Edition 2025 by Kingdom Publishers, London, UK.

You can purchase copies of this book from any leading bookstore or at:
www.kingdompublishers.co.uk

Contents

Acknowledgements	7
Introduction	9
My Story	10
Chapter 1 Why The 1611 King James Version?	21
Chapter 2 Trust	55
Chapter 3 What You Believe Is Limited By What You Know	116
Chapter 4 Let's Get Controversial!	176
Chapter 5 The End Times	248

Acknowledgements

First and foremost, I want to give thanks to God, whose grace, love, and faithfulness have been the guiding force behind this book. Without His Hand at work in my life, none of this would have been possible and I would have gotten lost in the distractions of this world.

To my beloved wife, Dede, your unwavering love, encouragement, and patience with me have been my anchor. Your steadfast faith and gentle spirit have been a constant reminder of God's goodness in my life. Thank you for walking with me through every season and being my greatest support as I pursued this calling, while ignoring other things!

To my children, you are a blessing beyond words. Your joy, curiosity, and faith have continually inspired me to trust God more deeply. I pray this book serves as a testimony of that trust and a legacy of faith for you.

A special thank you to my dear friend, David. The first Christian I met who was ready with answers and encouraged me to explore the topic of faith. Instead of telling me, encouraged me, to investigate for myself. I can honestly say that without our friendship, this investigation into what is true would likely never have started. Your friendship was a source of strength, wisdom, and accountability throughout this journey. Thank you for putting up with me in my darkest moments and showing me a better path. I could not be more grateful for showing a genuine interest in my life. I look forward to meeting you again in the Kingdom of Heaven.

I also want to express my deep gratitude to the bible teachers, who have come into my life over the years, both in person and over the internet. Your insights, and dedication to the Word have shaped my understanding of trusting God and helped lay the foundations for this book. Your influence is woven into every chapter, and I am forever grateful for you forcing me to confront my own biases and making me rethink my worldview, where it came from and how to look through a different set of lenses. A special thank you to Kent Hovind of Creation Science Evangelism (www.drdino.com) for allowing me to use various pictures from your seminar which will be cited as 'Taken from CSE'. I can honestly say that it was this seminar that caused me to start my investigation into what I believed and why I believed it. Conducting that investigation for myself has completely changed the course of my life for the better and led me to Christ and the need to trust in Him.

Introduction

In a world filled with uncertainty, fear, and doubt, the need for trust has never been more pressing. Each day, we face challenges through personal struggles, societal upheavals, and global chaos, all of which test our sense of security. Yet, amid all of this, there remains a constant source of unwavering strength and hope: God.

This book is an exploration of what it truly means to trust God, not just in moments of triumph but in the valleys of despair. Trusting God goes beyond a simple belief in His existence; it requires surrender, faith, and a deep conviction that He is in control, even when life feels uncontrollable. It's about learning to let go of the need to understand everything, and instead resting in the assurance that God's plans are good, especially when we cannot see the full picture.

Throughout these pages, we will journey through scripture, testimonies, practical knowledge and wisdom to discover how to develop a trust in God that anchors through life's storms. Whether you are seeking to deepen your faith or struggling with doubt, my hope is that this book will encourage you to lean on God more fully and find peace in His presence.

Trusting God is not a one-time decision but a daily commitment to walk by faith, and not by sight. It's a relationship built over time, one that transforms our hearts and minds. As we open this book, let's invite God into the process, allowing Him to strengthen our trust and guide us closer to Him.

My Story

'Everybody wants to go to Heaven, but nobody wants to die.'

It never ceases to amaze me the number of times I ask both Christians and non-Christians alike, why they believe what they do, always surprised that there are not many that have really given the question a great deal of thought. Atheists believe that the Earth formed over millions of years from an explosion from nothing, yet do not seem to realise the shocking amount of faith that really requires.

Christians, likewise, believe many different things, from Young and Old Earth Creation, God is a Trinity, etcetera. When I started on my faith journey, I didn't convert for the longest time as many Christians didn't have a satisfactory answer for me. So many failed with the biblical command found in 1 Peter 3:15 – "But sanctify the Lord God in your hearts: and **be ready always to give an answer to every man that asketh you a reason of the hope that is in you with meekness and fear.**"

It is a good idea for Christians to follow the advice in the scriptures:

[25] "I applied mine heart to know, and to search, and to seek out wisdom, and the reason of things, and to know the wickedness of folly, even of foolishness and madness" (Ecclesiastes 7:25 KJV)

And

[15] "Study to shew thyself approved unto God, a workman that needeth not to be ashamed, rightly dividing the word of truth." (2 Timothy 2:15 KJV)

The Christians I speak to, even to this day, say they trust God yet have a shocking amount of their faith and belief in what the world teaches, and not so much what the Word says. The two are not compatible. In fact, the world says the complete opposite of the Word.

I was born in England to parents who thought they had no religious beliefs. My mother was very particular in allowing my siblings and myself to draw our own conclusions. Something I would later appreciate. I grew up in a standard environment for most kids in the Southeast of England. I went to public schools and was taught all the curriculum, as was the norm. It wasn't until I started working in engineering that I started questioning things, and until then, evolution was my go-to worldview. Although my schools did touch on religions of various faiths they didn't go to any kind of depth and were more top of the iceberg.

One thing that does happen when you question things is that you will quickly bring about a hornet's nest, once you not only challenge someone's worldview but also the accepted beliefs of society. Most people simply haven't really thought about why they believe what they do. Question further and you'll find that in most cases, their beliefs are rooted in teachings from things being taught as children or something that makes them feel good, and few seem to deviate from those beliefs.

But don't take my word for it. Try asking such questions with people you know, with whom you can have a conversation without it turning into an argument and/or the need to be right, and really listen to the answers. In many cases, even when evidence is provided to answer their questions many will hold to their beliefs. It is also ironic that, as a once proud evolutionist myself, I would say things like, it has been proven by carbon dating, etcetera without really thinking it through. I would later find out that was my ego talking! The ego, also known as our personality, only really cares about two things. Looking good and being right, and can have devastating consequences and lasting impacts if we are not willing to stop and look within at why some things make us think and feel the way we do.

Once I learnt to let go of my ego and look at something with a more critical eye, it helped me grow both spiritually, and as an individual. This book isn't here to preach to any particular group, it is merely here to challenge your thought process and provide some knowledge as to why you can trust the Bible 100% (well the KJV version at least, more on that later) and put all of your faith in God's Word over what the world tells you.

My dad was a policeman during my youth, and I remember him telling me to question everything. You'll be amazed at what people will lie about to make themselves look good or to avoid accountability and punishment. (Similarly, the three main motivating factors when a crime is committed boils down to three things - power, money and sex).

I had fully accepted evolution as a fact, as that is what I had been taught and hadn't questioned what I had been taught. It couldn't be wrong, could it? In my journey, I discovered that at many times throughout history, the majority has a reputation for being wrong! The majority followed Aaron into rebellion and not into the promised land!

My personal favourite example of this is Ignaz Phillipp Semmelweis, a Hungarian physician and scientist, known as the saviour of mothers. He was shocked that the women in his hospital in the doctors' wards had three times the mortality rate of the midwives' wards. In the 19th century, many women died of puerperal fever (also known as childbed fever) and as many as 30% of the women died giving birth.

Upon investigation, he found that the doctors in his hospital would examine a dead body and then go and see the next expecting mother. He insisted that the doctors in his hospital were to wash their hands after examining a dead body. The mortality rate dropped to below 2%. He published a book on his findings, 'Ethology, Concept and Prophylaxis of Childbed Fever'. But despite the results and the publications of his findings, this went against all the established scientific and medical opinions of the time, and his ideas were rejected by the community.

He could offer no theoretical explanation for these findings and was openly mocked by the doctors and professionals of the day. He became increasingly outspoken about his findings, with his reward for this incredible discovery, leading to his dismissal. Three hospitals in a row fired him for insisting that doctors wash their hands after examining a dead body. He eventually ended up in an asylum where he was then murdered. It wasn't until many years later that Louis Pasteur confirmed the Germ Theory, proving Ignaz correct. Ironically 3000 years earlier God told Moses in multiple verses in the book of Leviticus that if you touch any dead thing you are unclean and shall wash your clothes and bathe in water before you touch anybody else.

(KJV) Leviticus 5:2

[2] "Or if a soul touch any unclean thing whether it be a carcase of unclean cattle, or the carcase of unclean creeping things, and if it be hidden from him; he also shall be unclean and guilty."

(KJV) Leviticus 11:24-25:

[24] "And for these ye shall be unclean: whosoever toucheth the carcase of them shall be unclean until the even.

²⁵ And whosoever beareth ought of the carcase of them shall wash his clothes, and be unclean until the even."

(KJV) Leviticus 15:10:

¹⁰ "And whosoever toucheth any thing that was under him shall be unclean until the even: and he **that beareth any of those things shall wash his clothes, and bathe himself in water**, and be unclean until the even."

(KJV) Leviticus 17:15:

¹⁵ "And every soul that eateth that which died of itself, or that which was torn with beasts, whether it be one of your own country, or a stranger, he shall both wash his clothes, and bathe himself in water, and be unclean until the even: then shall he be clean."

We used to teach that if you were sick, you had bad or infected blood and would prescribe bloodletting or a course of leeches. George Washington died in this manner. In the same room where he was being bled to death there was a Bible which stated in Leviticus 17:11 – "For **the life of the flesh is in the blood:** and I have given it to you upon the altar to make an atonement for your souls: for it is the blood that maketh an atonement for the soul".

I also had no idea at the time that my worldview (and yours too) had major implications on how I lived my life and conducted myself as I went about my day. Then one day in 2005, I started a new apprenticeship in engineering, and it became obvious that even simple designs require a degree of thought. Over the course of many years how I saw the world began to change and when it did, my whole worldview began to fall apart, and so did my 'faith' in science/religion of Earth's formation.

I do have one caveat with regard to this book. I will only be referring to the King James Version (KJV) of the Bible, except for the specific part of the book as to why the KJV is the one I recommend you use. Many of the other versions have some issues that cannot be ignored. I'm sure the people who come up with the various versions of the Bible may have done so with good intentions. However, the love of money is the root of evil and to protect your work and obtain your copyright it must be different to the original with most working on a 10% rule. Otherwise, you do not get paid for your work. The NIV for example has over 200 verses MISSING. Even the New King James Version (NKJV) has a MAJOR problem in the book of Revelation. In the original 1611 KJV it reads:

(KJV) Revelation 13:16: 16 "And he causeth all, both small and great, rich and poor, free and bond, to receive a mark in their right hand, or in their foreheads:"

(NKJV) Revelation 13:16: 16 "He causes all, both small and great, rich and poor, free and slave, to receive a mark on their right hand or on their foreheads,"

Be honest. Did you catch it? Let's look again:

(KJV) Revelation 13:16: 16 "And he causeth all, both small and great, rich and poor, free and bond, to receive a mark in their right hand, or **in** their foreheads:"

(NKJV) Revelation 13:16: 16 "He causes all, both small and great, rich and poor, free and slave, to receive a mark on their right hand or **on** their foreheads,"

They have changed ONE letter which completely changes the context of the verse. 'On' could be something like wearing a glove, no big deal.

'IN' is something placed inside of you and thus not easily removed, such as a tattoo or microchip. This is a major problem.

Why does this bother me so much? Well, the Bible predicts in (KJV) 1 Timothy 4:

4 "Now the Spirit speaketh expressly, **that in the latter times some shall depart from the faith, giving heed to seducing spirits, and doctrines of devils;"**

This bothers me because the majority of Christians I meet believe we have now entered the latter days also known as the end times. I would agree, but some shall depart from the faith. Why?! After four years of praying on this, it has been firmly put on my heart, and a kick up the rear, that the reason they shall depart is because many Christians believe their faith foundation is stronger than it really is. They have one foot in what the world tells them and the other foot in God's Word. The two views are just not compatible, and with different translations of the Bible, it is no surprise to me some will get confused. There are many other reasons as we'll delve into this book. The different Bible versions play a factor. So, when they are challenged, they cannot provide answers. I had to write this book as said in James 2:26:

26 "For as the body without the spirit is dead, so faith without works is dead also."

This is my work in faith. Many claim to trust God, but in reality, they don't, not 100%. None of us do 100%. Some of that trust is in what the world teaches. Many are so stuck in what the world teaches that getting them to break their own prejudices and misconceptions will be a difficult undertaking. But with God, nothing is impossible. The biggest hurdle to obtaining the truth is the presumption that you already have it.

(KJV) Hosea 4:6: 6 **"My people are destroyed for lack of knowledge:** because thou has rejected knowledge, I will also reject thee, that thou shalt be no priest to me: seeing thou hast forgotten the law of thy God, I will also forget my children."

(KJV) Proverbs 3:5: 5 "Trust in the Lord with all thine heart; and lean not unto thine own understanding."

This book is to help strengthen your faith in God's Word and give you some knowledge so when times get tough, you will not depart from the faith and stay the course knowing it is trustworthy. You will be deeply rewarded in Heaven for doing so. The Bible says a just person walks by faith. But do not confuse faith with ignorance. Your faith should not be blind faith. We must not love the world, we are only a part of it. Remember the words of Jesus in John 15:18-22:

18 "If the world hate you, ye know that it hated me before it hated you.

19 If ye were of the world, the world would love his own: but because ye are not of the world, but I have chosen you out of the world, therefore the world hateth you.

20 Remember the word that I said unto you, The servant is not greater than his lord. If they have persecuted me, they will also persecute you; if they have kept my saying, they will keep yours also.

21 But all these things will they do unto you for my name's sake, because they know not him that sent me.

22 If I had not come and spoken unto them, they had not had sin: but now they have no cloak for their sin."

A good test to see how close to the Lord you are is to find out how much the world does not like you! Just mention online that marriage is between one man and one woman or that abortion is murder and see what comes back at you. Friendship with the world is enmity with God... When you truly have been born again it is evident in one's behaviour. You cannot go back to the old life, and are repentant should any of the old behaviours even try and creep in. Do you know what you need to do to end up in Hell? Absolutely nothing. Just be yourself and you'll get there just fine.

When I think of my own life before my salvation, I cannot return to those old behaviours. There is now an invisible barrier that prevents it. The devil knows how to tempt you but resist him, and he will flee from you. Why waste his time on someone who can resist when he could devour someone else?

Our faith is under constant attack in the world today. If you were to be arrested for being a Christian, would you be found innocent or guilty? Many throughout history have been killed for their faith in Jesus, known as Christian Martyrs. This means that they were found guilty just by being followers of Jesus. In some parts of the world today simply owning a Bible or gathering for worship is considered illegal. We may not face that in our Western countries, well not yet anyway, the question we need to ask is, can the way we live our lives show enough evidence of our faith in Jesus? Jesus specifically warns about this in Matthew 24:9-14:

[9] "Then shall they deliver you up to be afflicted, and shall kill you: and ye shall be hated of all nations for my name's sake.

[11] And then shall many be offended, and shall betray one another, and shall hate one another.

[12] And many false prophets shall rise, and shall deceive many.

[13] And because iniquity shall abound, the love of many shall wax cold.

¹⁴ But he that shall endure unto the end, the same shall be saved.

¹⁵ And this gospel of the kingdom shall be preached in all the world for a witness unto all nations; and then shall the end come."

Many shall be offended. In Psalm 119:165 it reads: "Great peace have they which love thy law: and <u>nothing shall offend them.</u>"

If the people are offended, they simply do not love God's law. That is what it says. Nothing written in this book should offend you. If you feel offended, may I humbly suggest that you examine your heart friend, and take it to the Lord in prayer.

Note that Jesus also says they shall betray one another. People WILL betray you if you openly put your faith in Jesus. Remember that Peter denied him three times, and James his brother doubted too. It wasn't until they had seen the risen Lord that they went to the grave, solidified in the faith. They saw Him risen. Remember, 'Blessed are those who have not seen yet have believed.'

The purpose of this book is to demonstrate that the Bible is not only true but more reliable than it first appears, especially to new Christians. It's just a case of putting the pieces together. It has, by design, hidden the clues in plain sight for anyone willing to ask for the eyes to see and ears to hear, and willing to put the time in.

Persecution is not a popular sermon over the prosperity gospel in so many churches today. Yet the Bible warns against persecution of the Lord's people, more so than prosperity and blessings. I've seen far too many sermons where the church leaders seem to be more interested in filling their churches than seeing souls in heaven, telling people what they want to hear and not what they NEED to hear.

Teaching the love of Christ 100% of the time and omitting the coming judgment. Both are important, yet God's grace, mercy, and patience will expire at some point. When Christ came the first time it was as a loving gentle servant. The second time will be to rule with a rod of iron, as mentioned in Psalm 2:9, Revelation 2:27, 12:5, and 19:15. We should preach and teach the love of Christ, but we must not miss out on the parts we don't like so much. The Bible warns this will happen in (KJV) 2 Timothy 4:3:

[3] **"For the time will come when they will not endure sound doctrine; but after their own lusts shall they heap to themselves teachers, having itching ears;"**

The question isn't what the Bible says. The real question is: Do you actually BELIEVE what it says over what the world tells you?

I have not met every one of you. I want to take this opportunity to say this book is in love and that I only want what is best for the reader because I care about your soul. I am also a sinner, just like everyone else, more so in many ways. Everyone is in a different stage in their walk with God and iron sharpens iron. Celebrate the wins and focus on the relationship with God. Rules without relationships lead to rebellion, relationships must be built FIRST, so those you interact with know you have their best interests at heart. I cannot build those relationships with you over a book. God has given us boundaries not to restrict us, but to protect us, often from ourselves.

Biblical Christianity is unpopular, while popular Christianity is unbiblical.

With that said let's dive in...

Chapter 1
Why The 1611 King James Version?

Before we begin, I need to clarify why I read the King James Version (KJV) out of the hundreds of different Bible versions. There are several reasons why we should only use the KJV and whole books have been written purely about this topic, so I won't go heavily into it as it has been addressed in other works. But I'll put some of my reasons why and would encourage you to go and investigate this for yourself.

I have heard it said that this issue is something that gets Christians to argue about minor things. I would lovingly disagree. I disagree because the Bible says some shall depart the faith, I believe it is the other versions that are a contributor to the issue. God promised to preserve his words. I would like to see them. Where are the preserved words for us English speakers? After a lot of study, I've come to the conclusion his words have indeed been preserved, in the 1611 KJV.

Before we continue, if you have accepted Christ as your saviour, we are brothers and sisters in Christ, 100% regardless of which version you read. I am merely trying to highlight the problems, demonstrate why the words matter and highlight why you should consider moving over to the KJV. Let us use the example in the introduction. When the mark of the beast comes along and you only read the NKJV, you may just think it is on the right hand or forehead, you may not think twice before taking something inside of you, like a microchip or tattoo, because it doesn't say in the right hand or forehead, therefore, it cannot be the 'mark'.

These small details change the context of the verses and that makes a big difference. As previously mentioned I am an engineer. The details really do matter. Even cheap furniture has a tolerance to put it together correctly. When I was working for a gear company, a one-tooth difference in a sprocket or gear could massively impact the way a gearbox or vehicle worked. You can try this for yourself. Try changing the gearing on your bicycle, you'll notice it behaves differently in each gear. The same is true in your car. Pull away in first, then again in second. You'll feel the difference. This is no accident; the different gears are to achieve different results. The same is true for our human behaviour. By changing what you read, watch, listen to, and all around consume, you change the way you live your life and ultimately how you behave. But more on that in a later chapter.

As touched on in the introduction to obtain a copyright and in turn protect your work, the writing must be different from the original with many working on a 10% rule, although, there is no specific percentage or clear-cut rule that determines how much a work needs to differ from an existing work to avoid infringement. However, it does need to differ, or you cannot claim your copyright and ultimately your money for your work. So many of these versions have been changed and even that Revelation example, has fallen out of tolerance. Remember the LOVE of money is the root of all evil. I cannot stress that enough, having lots of money isn't evil. The love of it is. A generic statement you can find in most versions of the Bible goes as follows:

"Use of up to 1000 verses from the ***** Bible is free, provided they do not comprise a whole book, nor more than 50% of the work.

The King James is Crown Copyrighted in the UK while being public domain for the rest of the world."

To be able to trust the Lord, you need to know his words, many of these other versions have made some serious errors in what the manuscripts say, so they do not infringe copyright and to get their money for their 'translation'.

A Bit of History

Once Christ had departed to heaven the disciples were writing their books and moving off to spread the gospel message. Persecution then came for the church for the next 1000 years or so, trying to stop the spread of the Gospel. If the Christians were caught, they were killed and their Bibles burnt. The Bibles were being copied and spread out. With no printing press, each copy would take roughly a year to reproduce with the quill dipped into the ink and then onto the paper.

In the 1500s and 1600s once persecution was no longer a major issue, the Christians then met and brought their copies of the manuscripts from all over the world, what is now the Bible. The five thousand copies of the Bible that had survived the persecution were then compared and were identical in all, but the spelling of people's names. God did preserve his Word as promised. It was then translated into English, which is where we get the King James Version.

Many of these copies would not have been side by side for hundreds of years with people of all nations making copies by hand. There are only two Bibles in the world. One is known as the majority text, which is where the KJV comes from and is derived from the 5000 manuscripts brought together once the persecution had calmed down. There are now 64,000 manuscripts available that support the KJV. When the KJV was translated there were only 5000. Only three manuscripts and 46 fragments support what is known as the

Alexandrian version, which is where we get the New International Version (NIV), Amplified (AMP), Good News Bible (GNB), English Standard Version (ESV) etcetera.

The Alexandrians were a group of people in Egypt who did not believe in the deity of Jesus Christ or his bodily resurrection, and subsequently made their version of the Bible making 6000 changes by changing the parts they didn't like. The only time the Alexandrians are mentioned in the Bible is when they are disputing with Stephen in Acts 6:9, arguing with the real Christians. Note that the only mention of them in the scripture is negative! Many respected church leaders such as Origen Adamantius, Jerome, and Augustine had many beliefs which are at odds with orthodox Christianity, then made copies of their version of the Bible which survived the persecution, but with their changes still in it. Three of these still survive today. One can be found in the Vatican library called the Codex Vaticanus. One was found in Alexandria, Egypt, and the third in a monastery called the Codex Sinaiticus. None of these three manuscripts agree with each other nor do they agree with the other 5000 manuscripts. As previously mentioned the 5000 manuscripts DO agree with each other. Monks then translated these three Alexandrian manuscripts into Latin, known as the Latin Vulgate. The vulgate is a good translation of the manuscripts, it's just a shame the manuscripts themselves had been altered. They had made a good translation of a bad manuscript! The Catholics then translated the Vulgate into English. These three manuscripts were older than the other 5000 manuscripts which survived the persecution. Older doesn't mean better though. If you are constantly using something, it eventually wears out and you need to replace it. Those manuscripts which were not destroyed would need to be re-written at some point to keep it fresh.

Then in the 1800s, two men, Brooke Wescott and Fenton Hort, took the three manuscripts believing that these manuscripts were older so must be better, right? They then combined the text into one Greek manuscript and sold it in 1881 saying they were the oldest and best manuscripts for translation. Well, the oldest copies known to survive anyway. The Revised Standard is the first English translation of this Greek manuscript. It is an excellent translation but of altered texts.

The other translations come from the Westcott and Hort such as the NIV, Good News, the English Standard Version (ESV), and AMP as well as many others, all come from this altered version. Many of them I am sure are translating it with good intentions. There is an old saying that the road to hell is paved with good intentions. But they are translating the wrong book.

God has promised to preserve his words. In (KJV) Psalm 12:6-7:

6 "The words of the LORD are pure words: as silver tried in a furnace of earth, purified seven times.

7 Thou shalt keep them, O LORD, thou shalt preserve them from this generation for ever."

It is pretty clear in this Psalm that God is telling us he will preserve his words. Well, what does the NIV say?

(NIV)

6 And the words of the LORD are flawless, like silver purified in a crucible, like gold refined seven times.

7 You, LORD, **will keep the needy safe and will protect us forever from the wicked,**

In the KJV verse 7 talks about preserving the word of God. Where on earth did the NIV get the protect the needy safe and protect us from wicked people from?! It does not say the same thing and does not pass my tolerance test! The verses that haven't been removed have verses that mean something completely different!

Use of Words

I am an engineer and have been most of my working life. Believe me when I tell you the small details REALLY DO MATTER. Why? Let's have a look at Genesis 3:3: Eve is telling the serpent that they can eat of the fruit of the trees except one, "God hath said, Ye shall not eat of it, neither shall ye touch it, lest ye die." But in verse 1 the serpent asked "Yea, hath God said,..."

Pay close attention. He literally swapped two words around to completely change the context from **God hath said to Hath God said?!** One is a command from the Lord, 'You shall not', and the other is a question to sow seeds of doubt in Eve. Did God really say that? The use of words cannot be overlooked as they change contexts and meaning just by rearranging the words.

'Words are like spells, it is why it is called spelling!'
Bruce Lee

If I ask you to make a cabinet two meters high, by four meters wide and four meters in length. Simple enough. But the two was meant to be a three. Now we have something that looks and fits differently to the original design intent. It might not even fit into the space it was meant for. In engineering we often use Geometric dimensioning & tolerancing or GD&T. It isn't uncommon to see images such as:

⌀ 1.50±.03

⊕ | ⌀ .005 | A   This image highlights the diameter of the hole to be 1.50 + or − 0.03 and a hole position tolerance of 0.005 to Datum A. For those not engineering minded this means that the hole can be a diameter of 1.47 to 1.53. No smaller and no bigger. That hole also cannot be out of position by 0.005 either. If it does not meet these tolerances the component will not mate with the mating part. Jesus himself said this in (KJV) Matthew 5:17-18:

17 "Think not that I am come to destroy the law, or the prophets: I am not come to destroy, **but to fulfil.**

18 For verily I say unto you, **Till heaven and earth pass, one jot or one tittle shall in no wise pass from the law, till all be fulfilled."**

A jot (Yod in Hebrew) or a tittle (A tittle is a small mark that distinguishes two letters such as O and Q) for English speakers is the equivalent of the old saying, 'Crossing of the T's and dotting of the I's'. Jesus Himself points out the small details matter.

The mark here is a tittle.

So what about Bible tolerance? There has to be a tolerance when these other versions come into being. Without it, you simply cannot put the Bible together the way we are supposed to. You may get the underlying message, but piecing it together becomes very difficult. One of the many reasons why so many will fall away is because the other Bible versions fall out of tolerance. Let's have a look at what I mean.

Genesis 27:39-40:

(KJV) ³⁹ "And Isaac his father answered and said unto him, Behold, thy **dwelling shall be** the fatness of the earth, and of the dew of heaven from above;"

(NIV) ³⁹ "His father Isaac answered him, Your **dwelling will be away from the earth's richness**, away from the dew of heaven above."

In these verses, the KJV states the dwelling shall be vs. the NIV which states dwelling away. It says the exact opposite.

Hosea 11:12:

(KJV) ¹² "Ephraim compasseth me about with lies, and the house of Israel with deceit: **but Judah yet ruleth with God**, and is faithful with the saints."

(NIV) ¹² "Ephraim has surrounded me with lies, Israel with deceit. **And Judah is unruly against God**, even against the faithful Holy One."

In this example from the book of Hosea in the KJV, it clearly states that Judah ruled with God. The NIV again says the complete opposite! My first Bible, the GNB also has a similar statement stating the people of Judah are still rebelling against, the faithful and holy God. These other two translations are saying the complete opposite of the KJV. Why? Because they are translated from the altered Alexandrian manuscripts. A good translation of a bad manuscript. Let us look at another.

Proverbs 18:24:

(KJV) 24 "A man that hath friends must shew himself friendly: and there is a friend that sticketh closer than a brother. "

(ESV) 24 "A man of many companions may come to ruin, but there is a friend who sticks closer than a brother."

In this example, the KJV makes it clear that if you want to have friends you must show yourself as friendly. But the ESV says you may come to ruin. You can come to ruin with just one bad friend!

Let's look at another.

In Matthew 18:11:

(KJV) 11 "For the Son of man is come to save that which was lost."

(NIV, GNB & ESV)

??? It's missing.

This verse is just outright missing from these other three versions. Why? Because they are translations of the Alexandrian manuscripts, and one of the verses that was removed in the 6000 changes they made. Some Bibles even put a footnote stating this verse was added by later translations. This is simply not correct. Their version took it out! Ask yourself, if another version added it, then why do these versions jump from verse 10 to 12? Surely, they should go from 10 to 11.

Many of the other versions have also removed the blood and the deity of Christ. The NIV has removed over 200 verses. This is a problem.

Let us look at (KJV) Acts 8:37:

37 "And Philip said, If thou believest with all thine heart, thou mayest. And he answered and said, I believe that Jesus Christ is the Son of God."

This verse is missing from both the NIV and the Good News! Why? Because the Alexandrians took issue with Jesus Christ being the Son of God. Some other versions may even come with a footnote stating this was added in by later versions, but just as above this is not correct. It was the earlier manuscripts that were the ones who removed it, and again if that really was the case, why jump from verse 36 to 38? Why not just call it 36 to 37?

Is it any wonder some Christians shall depart from the faith?

2 Timothy 2:15:

(KJV) 15 "**Study** to shew thyself approved unto God, a workman that needeth not to be ashamed, rightly dividing the word of truth."

(NASB) 15 "Be **diligent** to present yourself approved to God as a worker who [a]does not need to be ashamed, accurately handling the word of truth."

Study means to be engaged in learning by observation and research. Diligent means to be careful and persevering in carrying out duties. Again, these two verses mean completely different things! We as Christians should be studying! The course of my studies is the reason this book exists. If we do not take the time to study, we can be easily deceived.

The more you know about scientific discoveries and the state of the world today, the more comfortable the Bible reads. Study, or a lack of it, is one of the reasons some shall depart from the faith. Friends, I encourage you to study! This life of ours today is short. We do not know if we will have our appointment with God at age 20 or 80. But I can promise you one thing. Eternity is longer and you will not be late for your appointment!

We need to be studying to provide answers for those who seek reasons to believe and to solidify our own faith for when the tough times come. This does not mean you need to know everything, if we were to cover every single objection, this book would be ten times bigger than the Bible! But we must make a point of studying.

One of the many things we need to take notice of is the words that are used. It's a real shame that the New King James Version (NKJV) couldn't get the translation from the KJV correct! Some people say the KJV is hard to read and it is at first. But once you get used to it, it becomes easy. Like most things in life, it gets easier the more you do something. Everything is hard the first time. Words in the KJV like 'readith' should be self-explanatory in the context of the verse you happen to be reading.

In the original 1611 KJV, the English people were not using words like, 'how art thou'? But some words in the English language can be a pain. Let's take the word 'You' as an example. If I were speaking to a group of people and said, 'You come with me'. Do I mean an individual or a group? The translators used words like 'ye' and 'thou' as they are a bit more distinct. If the word starts with a 'Y' such as 'ye', it is plural, if it is 'TH' like 'thou', 'thine', then it is singular. Now when Jesus says in (KJV) John 3:7:

7 "Marvel not that I said unto **thee, Ye** must be born again. – Now it makes a bit more sense. I'm telling you (singular) that you (plural) must be born again."

Many versions also edit the Genesis versions from THE first day to ONE day. This is because some of the translators do not believe in a literal six-day creation and are trying to say that the world is billions of years old when there is a shocking amount of evidence that suggests that isn't the case, but that isn't taught in the schools. Only one option is. This is not teaching a person to think critically. That teaches someone, what to think and, not how to think. God made it clear that he made the world in six days.

In Exodus (KJV) 20:11:

[11] "For in **six days** the LORD made heaven and earth, the sea, and all that in them is, and rested the seventh day: wherefore the LORD blessed the sabbath day, and hallowed it. – I think God is trying to make it clear it was made in six literal days and rested on the seventh. Not because he needed a rest, but more to structure our week. It is we as humans who need rest. Ask any athlete and they will tell you how important the rest part is."

Again, in (KJV) Exodus 31:17:

[17] "It is a sign between me and the children of Israel for ever: for in **six days** the LORD made heaven and earth, and on the seventh day he rested, and was refreshed."

And again, in (KJV) Hebrews 4:4:

[4] "For he spake in a certain place of the seventh day on this wise, And God did rest the seventh day from all his works."

God makes it clear he made it all in six days. In several versions, they replace the first day with one day. Why? In the English dictionary the word 'the' is described as the definite article. The answer is simple, they do not believe in a literal six-day creation. Remember, the details matter. Also, consider that if it really were millions of years old, then death would come before sin. When the Bible clearly teaches that death came into the world because of man's sin.

See Romans 5:12:

(KJV) Genesis 1:5: 5 "And God called the light Day, and the darkness he called Night. And the evening and the morning were **the first day**."

(NASB) Genesis 1:5: 5 "God called the light "day," and the darkness He called "night." And there was evening and there was morning, **one day**."

The irony is that these other versions who say one day in Genesis are trying to get out of the literal six days of creation, yet if you go to Exodus 31:17 it still states he made it all in six days in all of the other versions I have looked at.

God promised to preserve his word, He did not promise to preserve how we speak or use our language. As an example, 50 years ago, the word 'gay' meant happy, 'sick' meant unwell, and 'cool' was something that wasn't hot. Those words have had some extra definitions added since then. Many words have either added additional definitions since the KJV was first translated or the entire definition has changed completely!!

Let's look at the very start of the Bible when God tells Adam to replenish the earth. The word replenish means to fill up again, right?

Genesis 1:28:

(KJV) 28 "And God blessed them, and God said unto them, Be fruitful, and multiply, and **replenish** the earth, and subdue it: and have dominion over the fish of the sea, and over the fowl of the air, and over every living thing that moveth upon the earth."

Today the word 'replenish' means to fill again to former fullness. But when the 1611 KJV was translated its primary definition was to fill. In 1650 a second definition was added, which was to refill.

> **REPLEN'ISH**, *v. t.* [Norm. *replener*, to fill; It. *riempire*; L. *re* and *plenus*, full.]
> 1. To fill; to stock with numbers or abundance. The magazines are *replenished* with corn. The springs are *replenished* with water.
>
> Multiply and *replenish* the earth. Gen. i.
>
> 2. To finish; to complete. [*Not in use.*]
> Shak.
>
> **REPLEN'ISH**, *v. i.* To recover former fullness.
> Bacon.
>
> **REPLEN'ISHED**, *pp.* Filled; abundantly supplied.

Image taken from CSE.

For hundreds of years, the word 'replenish' only meant to fill. In an 1828 (above) dictionary the primary definition is fill.

> **RE-PLEN'ISH**, *v. t.* [Norm. *replener*, to fill; It. *riempire*; L. *re* and *plenus*, full.]
> 1. To fill; to stock with numbers or abundance. The magazines are *replenished* with corn; the springs are *replenished* with water.
>
> Multiply and *replenish* the earth. — Gen. 1.
>
> 2. To finish; to complete. [*Not in use.*] Shak.
>
> **RE-PLEN'ISH**, *v. i.* To recover former fullness.

Image taken from CSE.

Above is an 1891 dictionary.

> **Re-plen′ish** (rē-plĕn′Ĭsh), *v. t.* [R<small>EPLENISHED</small> (-plĕn′isht); R<small>EPLENISHING</small>.] <u>To fill up again;</u> <u>to fill completely.</u>

Image taken from CSE.

In 1892, just one year later, the dictionary switched the definitions, now replenish primary definition was to fill again.

> **re‑plen‑ish** (ri plen′ish) *vt.* < L. *re-*, again + *plenus*, full 1 <u>to make full or complete again</u> 2 to supply again —**re‑plen′ish‑ment** *n.*

Image taken from CSE.

In 1989 the definition changed again and now only means to fill again. They removed what was the original primary definition of the word.

The Collins dictionary I have in my house under the word 'replenish' doesn't even mention fill. This small, but important, detail leaves many people thinking that maybe there were people before Adam, when the Bible clearly teaches that Adam was the first man.

The word DRAGON - is featured over 30 times in the Bible. When the 1611 KJV was translated the word 'dinosaur' was not in the English dictionary. It hadn't been thought of yet! The word 'dinosaur' was invented by Sir Richard Owen in 1841. Before that, they were known as dragons. There are plenty of legends of dragons throughout history. St. George is famous for killing a dragon, the Welsh flag is a dragon, while the Chinese calendar features 11 real animals and one mythical one. Question...when the Chinese calendar was first produced, could there have been 12 real animals? What we would call a 'dinosaur' was called a 'dragon' by our ancestors. You will not find the word 'dinosaur' in the Bible as the word hadn't been thought about yet.

In 1891, the word 'dinosaur' is still missing from this American dictionary below:

```
DIN'ING-HALL, n.   A hall for a company to dine in.
DIN'ING-ROOM, n.   A room for a family or for com-
    pany to dine in;  a room for entertainments
DIN'ING-TA'BLE, n.   A table used for the purpose
    of dining.
DIN'NED, pp.   Stunned with a loud noise.
DIN'NER, n.   [Fr. diner;  It. dinare.  See DINE.]
    1. The meal taken about the middle of the day;
    or the principal meal of the day, eaten between noon
    and evening.
    2. An entertainment;  a feast.
        Behold, I have prepared my dinner. — Matt. xxii.
DIN'NER-LESS, a.   Having no dinner.       Fuller.
DIN'NER-TA'BLE, n.   A table at which dinner is
    taken.
DIN'NER-TIME, n.   The usual time of dining.  Pope.
DI-NO-THE'RI-UM, n.   [Gr. δεινος, terrible, and
    θηριον, beast.]
        A gigantic, herbivorous, aquatic animal, fifteen or
    eighteen feet long;  now extinct.  [See DERMOTHE-
    RIUM.]                                 Buckland.
DINT, n.   [Sax. dynt, a blow or striking.  It may be
    connected with din and ding.]
    1. A blow;  a stroke.                    Milton.
    2. Force;  violence;  power exerted;  as, to win by
    dint of arms, by dint of war, by dint of argument or
```

Image taken from CSE.

Next is a 1946 dictionary that states, dragon, 1. Now rare:

> **dragon** 3
>
> **drag'on** (drăg'ŭn), n. [OF., fr. L. *draco*, *-onis*, fr. Gr. *drakōn*.] 1. *Now Rare.* A huge serpent. 2. A fabulous animal, generally a monstrous winged scaly serpent, lizard, or saurian. 3. A fierce or very strict person, esp. a woman; a duenna. 4. Any of several plants of the arum family popularly associated with dragons. 5. A word used in the Authorized Version to translate several Hebrew forms, some of which are translated by *jackal* or *serpent* in the Revised Version. 6. Formerly, a short musket. — Dragon, as represented in Heraldry.

Image taken from CSE.

The word 'unicorn' - In my Collins dictionary the word 'unicorn' today is defined as: 'Imaginary horse like creature with one horn growing from its forehead.'

The word 'unicorn' is used in the Bible nine times in Numbers, Deuteronomy, Job, Psalms and Isaiah. Because of that people will often scoff at you and say things like, 'If you believe in God, you must believe in unicorns.' Not realising, just like the word 'replenish', the word has changed meaning over time.

However, look inside an 1828 Webster dictionary below, the word 'unicorn' is explained as:

> **U'NICORN**, n. [L. *unicornis*; *unus*, one, and *cornu*, horn.]
> 1. An animal with one horn; the monoceros. This name is often applied to the rhinoceros.

It does not mention a horse or a horse-like animal. Neither does it say mythical. But it does say 'often applied to the rhinoceros.' In the same dictionary under rhinoceros:

> RHINOC'EROS, n. [Fr. *rhinoceros* or *rhinocerot*; It. Sp. *rinoceronte*; L. *rhinoceros*; Gr. ρινοχερως, nose-horn; ρω, the nose, W. *rhyn*, a point, and χερας, a horn.] A genus of quadrupeds of two species, one of which, the *unicorn*, has a single horn growing almost erect from the nose. This animal when full grown, is said to be 12 feet in length. There is another species with two horns, the *bicornis*. They are natives of Asia and Africa. *Encyc.*

It was understood there were two distinct species of rhinos, one being a unicorn and the other as bicornis. In Asia, the one-horned Rhino is still referred to as the Rhinoceros Unicornis. The KJV was translated in 1611, 400 years ago, now. If the definition of unicorn has changed in just 200 years from the 1828 dictionary to now, it is foolish to use a modern definition of the word unicorn. Unicornis is a Latin word.

In (KJV) Psalm 92:10:

[10] "But my horn shalt thou exalt like the horn of an unicorn: I shall be anointed with fresh oil."

It is interesting that in the Latin Vulgate the same verse reads:

"Et excaltabitur sicut **unicornis** cornu meum, et senectus mea in misericordia uberi."

The Vulgate uses unicornis and so does the Asian One-Horned rhino. What is interesting however is if you then go to (KJV) Job 39:9:

⁹ "Will the unicorn be willing to serve thee, or abide by thy crib?"

The Vulgate reads:

"Numquid volet **rinoceros** servire tibi aut morabitur ad Praesepe tuum?"

I find it interesting that the Vulgate, like the Webster's dictionary, uses unicorn and rhino interchangeably. The Asian One-horned Rhino is described as Rhinoceros Unicornis. Very interesting! In fact, the words used in the Vulgate under the verses Numbers 23:22, Deuteronomy 33:17, Psalm 22:22, 29:6, 92:10, Job 39:9-10 and Isaiah 34:7 use five different words. They are:

Rinoceros,
Rinocerotis,
Rinocerta,
Unicornium
Unicornis.

All of which point to a one-horned rhino. However, the words used are changed based on the context of the verses in which they appear.

These five words are being used as one in the KJV as unicorn. In this instance, the Latin word 'unicornis' is being used and means a one-horned rhino, and as in 1611, the word 'unicorn' was understood to be a rhino, **not** a mythical horse from today's definition of the word.

There was a book published in 2003 by Eric Dinerstein called 'The Return of The Unicorns'. On the front cover, there is a picture of two rhinos. (Search it for yourself).

Also of interest is an extinct creature called the Elasmotherium Sibiricum, otherwise known as the 'Giant Unicorn'. It is suspected that this is the unicorn the Bible is referring to.

The word 'behemoth' – Is featured in Job, a lot of people believe this to be a hippo or an elephant. However, the scripture would suggest otherwise.

(KJV) Job 40:16- 17:

"Lo now, his strength is in his loins, and his force is in the navel of his belly.

He moveth his tail like a cedar: the sinews of his stones are wrapped together."

A cedar is a type of tree. Elephants and hippos do not have a tail that big! This could be something more like a brachiosaurus. It would at least fit the criteria.

In (KJV) Romans 1:13:

13 "Now I would not have you ignorant, brethren, that oftentimes I purposed to come unto you, (but **was let** hitherto,) that I might have some fruit among you also, even as among other Gentiles."

The word 'let' used to mean hindered. Today it means allowed.

Contradictions in the KJV Bible?

One of the things a believer will hear quite early on in their faith journey is that the Bible is full of contradictions. But is it? In the Alexandrian translations, you'll find many! How can you trust God's

Word if you find errors in it? What about the KJV though? Well, let us now address some of those and have a look at some of the most common rebuttals from non-believers and clear up some confusion.

IN GENESIS 10 IT STATES THAT THE LANGUAGES WERE DIVIDED UP, BUT ONE CHAPTER LATER IT SAYS THE WHOLE WORLD WAS OF ONE LANGUAGE. WHICH IS IT?

(KJV) Genesis 10:31:

31 "These are the sons of Shem by their clans and languages, in their territories and nations."

(KJV) Genesis 11:1:

1 "Now the whole world had one language and a common speech."

Genesis 11 is simply a recap of events, much like a headline of a story. When you read a headline, it tells you the essence of what happened and then goes into the details about how the incident got there. Not a contradiction.

HOW MANY PEOPLE DIED IN THE PLAGUE?

(KJV) Numbers 25:9:

9 "And those that died in the plague were **twenty and four thousand**."

(KJV) 1 Corinthians 10:8:

8 "Neither let us commit fornication, as some of them committed, and fell in one day **three and twenty thousand**."

Look again:

(KJV) Numbers 25:9:

⁹ "And **those that died in the plague** were twenty and four thousand."

(KJV) 1 Corinthians 10:8:

⁸ "Neither let us commit fornication, as some of them committed, **and fell in one day** three and twenty thousand."

24,000 people died in the plague, but 23,000 of them died in just one day. The remaining thousand died later. Not a contradiction. Pay attention to the words used.

HOW DID KING SAUL DIE?

(KJV) 1 Samuel 31:4-5:

⁴ "Then said Saul unto his armourbearer, Draw thy sword, and thrust me through therewith; lest these uncircumcised come and thrust me through, and abuse me. But **his armourbearer would not**; for he was sore afraid. **Therefore Saul took a sword, and fell upon it.**

⁵ And when his armourbearer saw that **Saul was dead,** he fell likewise upon his sword, and died with him."

(KJV) 1 Samuel 1:8-10:

⁸ "And he said unto me, Who art thou? And I answered him, I am an Amalekite.

⁹ He said unto me again, Stand, I pray thee, upon me, and slay me: for anguish is come upon me, because my life is yet whole in me.

¹⁰ So I stood upon him, and slew him, because I was sure that he could not live after that he was fallen: and I took the crown that was upon his head, and the bracelet that was on his arm, and have brought them hither unto my lord."

It should be obvious that this Amalekite is lying. Possibly to claim a reward and David's favour. It was no secret Saul and David had become enemies. Saul killed himself.

WHAT ABOUT SOLOMONS BATHS?

(KJV) 2 Chronicles 4:2:

² "Also he made a molten sea of **ten cubits** from brim to brim, round in compass, and five cubits the height thereof; and a line of **thirty cubits** did compass it round about."

If something is ten cubits across it isn't 30 cubits around. To find the circumference of a circle the formula is π * ⌀ = Circumference. It should be 31.145. How do we account for that?

Verse 5 says:

⁵ "And the **thickness** of it was an **handbreadth**, and the brim of it like the work of the **brim** of a cup, with flowers of lilies; and it received and held three thousand baths."

There are two theories to solve this. One says it was ten cubits outside to outside not counting the brass thickness. Take ten cubits (A cubit is elbow to fingertip) and subtract two handbreadths and calculate in reverse you'll get a value of π for the inner circumference.

The second theory is that with the brim of a cup, so 30 cubits around the bowl but ten cubits across brim to brim counting the lip that many cups have. See image below.

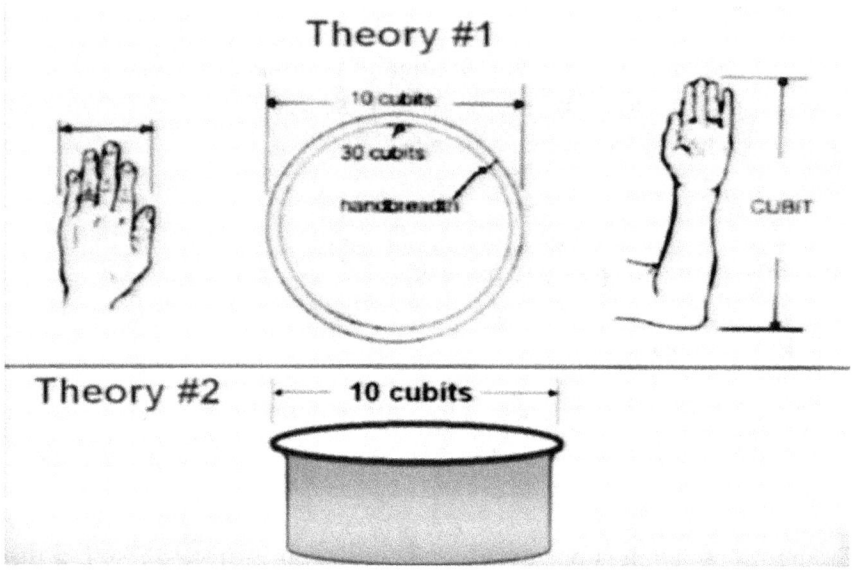

Image taken from CSE.

(KJV) 1 Kings 7:26:

26 "And it was an hand breadth thick, and the brim thereof was wrought like the brim of a cup, with flowers of lilies: it contained **two thousand baths**."

(KJV) 1 Chronicles 4:5:

5 "And the thickness of it was an handbreadth, and the brim of it like the work of the brim of a cup, with flowers of lilies; and it received and held **three thousand baths**."

Is it 2000 or 3000 baths? If you read it carefully, you'll notice in Kings, it says it CONTAINED two thousand baths. But in Chronicles it says HELD three thousand baths. It is simply two thirds full. It can hold 3000 but only has 2000. Remember the details matter.

HOW MANY HORSES DID SOLOMON HAVE?

(KJV) 1 Kings 4:26:

26 "And Solomon had **forty thousand stalls of horses for his chariots**, and twelve thousand horsemen."

(KJV) 1 Chronicles 9:25:

25 "And Solomon had **four thousand stalls for horses and chariots**, and twelve thousand horsemen; whom he bestowed in the chariot cities, and with the king at Jerusalem."

Kings say forty thousand stalls of horses FOR his chariots. This doesn't mention how many chariots he had; it only mentions how many horses he had FOR the chariots. Chronicles says four thousand stalls for horses AND chariots. Solomon had stalls where he would keep the horses and chariots and other stalls for the horses for the chariots. With forty thousand stalls for the horses and another four thousand stalls for his horses AND chariots that equates to ten horses per chariot.

The NIV and the GNB get this quite wrong. While the NASB gets it right:

Kings 4:26:

(NIV) 26 "Solomon had four thousand stalls for chariot horses, and twelve thousand **horses**."

(GNB) "Solomon had 40,000 stalls for his chariot horses and 12,000 cavalry **horses**."

NOT horsemen as written in the KJV, these other versions are just horses. Last time I checked, there was a difference between horses and horsemen!

Chronicles 9:25:

(NIV) 25 "Solomon had four thousand stalls for horses and chariots, and twelve thousand horses,[a] which he kept in the chariot cities and also with him in Jerusalem."

(GNB) 25 "King Solomon also had four thousand stalls for his chariots and horses, and had twelve thousand cavalry horses. Some of them he kept in Jerusalem **and the rest he stationed in various other cities.** - ??? The KJV only states they were with the king at Jerusalem. What are these other cities?"

HOW MANY MEN DID DAVID KILL?

(KJV) 2 Samuel 10:18:

18 "And the Syrians fled before Israel; and David slew the men of **seven hundred chariots** of the Syrians, and forty thousand horsemen, and smote Shobach the captain of their host, who died there."

(KJV) 1 Chronicles 19:18:

18 "But the Syrians fled before Israel; and David slew of the Syrians **seven thousand men which fought in chariots**, and forty thousand footmen, and killed Shophach the captain of the host."

Read it carefully! Men which <u>fought in</u> chariots. That makes ten men per chariot. Read what it says and not what you want it to say. Remember the details matter! This is another one the NIV gets wrong.

(NIV) 1 Samuel 10:18:

¹⁸ "But they fled before Israel, and David killed seven hundred of their charioteers and forty thousand of their foot soldiers. He also struck down Shobak the commander of their army, and he died there."

(NIV) 1 Chronicles 19:18:

¹⁸ "But they fled before Israel, and David killed seven thousand of their charioteers and forty thousand of their foot soldiers. He also killed Shophak the commander of their army."

WAS JONAH SWALLOWED BY A WHALE OR A FISH?

(KJV) Jonah 1:17:

¹⁷ "Now the LORD had prepared **a great fish** to swallow up Jonah. And Jonah was in the **belly of the fish** three days and three nights."

(KJV) Matthew 12:40:

⁴⁰ "For as Jonas was three days and three nights **in the whale's belly**; so shall the Son of man be three days and three nights in the heart of the earth."

This one with Jonah is something that has been lost to time. Today we make two different categories, but in the Biblical classification, a whale is classified as a fish. As would also be a shark, dolphin, etcetera. All of those are deemed as fish in the Bible.

One of the first Bibles I received was the Good News Bible. Now this version DOES contain contradictions. When I started reading through it and even at the early part of my faith journey, I spotted something off with this version.

LET ME ASK YOU A QUESTION, WHO KILLED GOLIATH? IF YOU SAID DAVID THEN WELL DONE. WHO KILLED GOLIATH'S BROTHER? NOW LET'S COMPARE THE TWO.

(KJV) 2 Samuel 21:19:

[19] "And there was again a battle in Gob with the Philistines, where Elhanan the son of Jaareoregim, a Bethlehemite, **slew the brother of Goliath** the Gittite, the staff of whose spear was like a weaver's beam."

(GNB) 2 Samuel 21:19:

[19] "There was another battle with the Philistines at Gob, **and Elhanan son of Jair** from Bethlehem **killed Goliath from Gath**, whose spear had a shaft as thick as the bar on a weaver's loom."

Sorry, who killed Goliath? This does not say the same thing.

To add insult to that in 1 Samuel 17:50 in the Good News Bible:

[50] "And so, without a sword, **David defeated and killed Goliath** with a sling and a stone!"

The Good News cannot even stay consistent from one book to the next!

Even in the example used in the introduction the GNB, in the book of Revelation, when talking about the mark of the beast, it is used on the right hand instead of in the right hand.

Many versions also leave out the fact that the blood of Jesus washes us from our sins. The word 'wash' is to clean. The word 'freed' is to release or liberate. Again this does not say the same thing.

In Revelation 1:5:

(KJV) 5 "**And from Jesus Christ**, who is the faithful witness, and the first begotten of the dead, and the prince of the kings of the earth. Unto him that loved us, and **washed us** from our sins in his own blood,"

(NIV) 5 "**And from Jesus Christ**, who is the faithful witness, the firstborn from the dead, and the ruler of the kings of the earth. To him who loves us and has **freed us** from our sins by his blood,"

Ephesians 3:9:

(KJV) 9 "And to make all men see what is the fellowship of the mystery, which from the **beginning of the world** hath been hid in God, who created all things **by** Jesus Christ"

(NKJV) 9 "And to make all see what *is* the fellowship of the mystery, which from the **beginning of the ages** has been hidden in God who created all things **through** Jesus Christ;"

(NIV) 9 "And to make plain to everyone the administration of this mystery, which for **ages past** was kept hidden in **God, who created all things**."

(GNB) 9 "And of making all people see how God's secret plan is to be put into effect. God, who is the Creator of all things, kept his secret **hidden through all the past ages**,"

The KJV says the beginning of the world, which is a set point in time and created BY Jesus Christ because Jesus is God in the flesh. Most of the other versions change it to ages and even remove Jesus Christ entirely as they are translated from the Alexandrian manuscripts who did not believe Jesus was God in flesh. The NKJV, kept Jesus in but all these other versions are trying really hard to suggest the world is millions of years old when it uses the word ages, implying it was made over millennia. Again, in Exodus 31:17 they all say he made the world in six days.

The DETAILS MATTER!

What about Easter? Easter is something that Christians celebrate as part of the resurrection of Christ. But Easter is actually a Pagan festival of Ishtar (Easter). It is to celebrate the earth regenerating after the winter months. This festival was always at the end of April with so many days after the full moon, this formula is still used today to get the dates for Easter. It's why the Easter holiday dates change year by year. Christians have just 'borrowed' the holiday!

In (KJV) Acts 12:4:

⁴ "And when he had apprehended him, he put him in prison and delivered him to four quaternions of soldiers to keep him; intending **after Easter** to bring him forth to the people."

Every other version of the Bible I have either read or checked says Passover, including the NKJV! To understand why the 1611 KJV states Easter we'll need to look back to, and understand, the original Passover.

In the KJV Acts 12:1-4:

"Now about that time Herod the king stretched forth his hands to vex certain of the church.

And he killed James the brother of John with the sword.

And because he saw it pleased the Jews, he proceeded further to take Peter also. **(Then were the days of unleavened bread.)**

And when he had apprehended him, he put him in prison, and delivered him to four quaternions of soldiers to keep him; intending **after Easter** to bring him forth to the people."

In (KJV) Exodus 12:1-3, (The month in verse 2 is April):

¹ "And the LORD spake unto Moses and Aaron in the land of Egypt saying,

² **This month shall be unto you the beginning of months: <u>it shall be the first month of the year</u> to**

<u>**you.**</u>

³ Speak ye unto all the congregation of Israel, saying, **In the tenth day of this month they shall take to them every man a lamb,** according to the house of their fathers, a lamb for an house"

(KJV) Exodus 12:6-8 KJV

⁶ **"And ye shall keep it up until the fourteenth day of the same month:** and the whole assembly of the congregation of Israel shall kill it in the evening.

⁷ And they shall take of the blood, and **strike it on the two side posts and on the upper door post of the houses**, wherein they shall eat it.

⁸ And **they shall eat the flesh in that night**, roast with fire, and unleavened bread; and with bitter herbs they shall eat it."

(KJV) Exodus 12:11

[11] "And thus shall ye eat it; with your loins girded, your shoes on your feet, and your staff in your hand; and ye shall eat it in haste: **it is the LORD's passover."**

(KJV) Exodus 12:14-15:

(KJV) [14] "And **this day shall be unto you for a memorial; and ye shall keep it a** feast to the LORD throughout your generations; ye shall keep it a feast by an ordinance for ever.

[15] **Seven days shall ye eat unleavened bread;** even the first day ye shall put away leaven out of your houses: for whosoever eateth leavened bread from the first day until the seventh day, that soul shall be cut off from Israel."

So, what's the procedure? On, the tenth day of April, you pick out a lamb and watch it for four days to ensure there are not any blemishes. On the 14th day, kill it, put the blood on the doorpost and eat it that night. For the next seven days you'll be on the run from Pharaoh, so you have to eat unleavened bread.

(KJV) Exodus 12:18:

[18] **"In the first month, on the fourteenth day of the month at even, ye shall eat unleavened bread, <u>until the one and twentieth day of the month</u> at even."** (Exodus 12:18)

From the 15th to the 21st eat unleavened bread.

(KJV) Numbers 28:16-17:

¹⁶ "And in **the fourteenth day** of the first month **is the passover** of the LORD.

¹⁷ And in **the fifteenth day of this month is the feast: seven days shall unleavened bread be eaten.**"

In Acts 12 it states that Peter was arrested during the days of unleavened bread, **which is <u>after</u> the**

Passover. The Passover had gone. Herod wanted to kill Peter during his pagan festival of Easter (Ishtar) which was some days away. By stating Easter in Acts 12:4 the KJV is the only Bible I am aware of that gets this correct!

Conclusion

As an engineer the details are paramount! Every assembly has a tolerance. If you read other versions and still get the overarching message of the gospel then fine, what happens though is that non-believers will try and trip you up on the parts that put the pieces together neatly. The Bible is 66 books penned by 40 people. Only the KJV has a tight tolerance. I humbly urge you to really study this topic.

It will be worth your time. Today we have incredible access to information at speed. There is the Holy Bible app where you can compare all of the different versions in a matter of minutes. A resource that wasn't there just 30 years ago. I hope I have provided you with some good reasons why you should consider a switch to the

KJV if you haven't already and enough information to make you a bit curious to explore for yourself.

It is an incredible shame that even the study Bibles and 'modern' translations have not crossed referenced with old dictionaries. It is part of the human condition to assume that some of these things, such as the meanings of words, have remained constant but that simply isn't the case. When conducting our own Bible study, it is important to consider some of these variables and address those that do not appear to make sense to us at first.

You can do quick comparisons between the Bible versions using www.biblegateway.com which is what I have used to compare many of these different versions.

Chapter 2
Trust

I want you to ask yourself something. On a scale of 0 – 100% how much would you say you trust God? I'd be willing to bet most Christians would say 100%. But that simply isn't true.

Trusting something or someone you have not seen can be difficult. That said I cannot see gravity, air, nor the laws of physics but I trust they are all present, neither can I see radio and microwaves. During a hurricane when you see all the debris flying around? It isn't the wind you are seeing. It is the damage the wind is doing that you see. God works in a similar fashion. You can see his handiwork in all of creation if you look for it, even though you do not see Him directly.

As a parent there have been many times, I have had to discipline my children because they are trying to do something that may harm them or others around them. When my daughter was able to reach our gas cooker knobs she tried to play with them, thinking the hissing sound was amusing. Dad did not find playing with the gas cooker very funny.

When I used to tell my son not to do something I would give him the 'death stare' and 99% of the time he would stop. My daughter on the other hand would just laugh at me. Literally laugh at me and do it anyway! Her punishment, she does not like to be restrained. Dad had to keep her seated in the naughty / time-out area for a few minutes, with her screaming in my face until she got the message that playing with the gas would not be acceptable. Those minutes felt a lot longer than they really were, but the result? She no longer touches the gas knobs. The message was received.

My son is currently into playing chess. Chess is an excellent game that replicates life more than you might think. The whole purpose of the game is to trap the king of the opposing side. Notice that the king doesn't get taken out of play. It is just checkmate with the king being unable to move. God and Satan are in a cosmic chess game. One thing you'll notice in chess is that it is unlikely to checkmate your opponent without taking some of the pieces in the process. In most cases, pieces must fall in order to trap the king. Each piece that is taken out still exists, it just no longer on the board. God and Satan have been trying to checkmate each other for a while.

Isaiah 14:12-15:

"How art thou fallen from heaven, O Lucifer, son of the morning! how art thou cut down to the ground, which didst weaken the nations!

For thou hast said in thine heart, I will ascend into heaven, I will exalt my throne above the stars of God: I will sit also upon the mount of the congregation, in the sides of the north:

I will ascend above the heights of the clouds; I will be like the most High."

Satan wants to be God and wants to be worshipped as God and he will be, for a time. The rise of the Anti-Christ will ensure that when he brings in the New World Order and one world religion.

But we know from scripture in Romans 8:28:

[28] "And we know that all things work together for good to them that love God, to them who are the called according to his purpose."

His purpose. Not ours. Notice it also says things work together for good. It does NOT say that everything that happens to you will be good though. Have you ever tried eating flour? What about a mouthful of sugar? Perhaps baking powder? Or even a drinking vanilla extract? And a large spoonful of butter and some raw eggs? Sounds disgusting right? But if you combine those and mix them up you can make a vanilla cake, which is great. The individual ingredients are disgusting on their own. The same is true with chapters of your life. Each chapter is unique, some chapters do not make sense. But combined?

The Bible too has an element of design to it. Individual books in the Bible don't make a lot of sense, the answers are found in one of the other books or by the combination of many. So, if some elements were removed the overall message is still intact. People who read the other Bible versions for example know that Jesus died for our sins, but the puzzle pieces have been mixed up or removed adding to confusion, but the message is still there.

Do I understand God's reasoning and purposes? No, not at all. Some things don't make sense, and we must, not lean on our own understanding. In my own life, there have been things that at one time seemed devastating where I felt broken, angry, enraged, and heartbroken. Such as my parents' separation in my early years, and the unexpected death of my dear friend and mentor, which all played a part. Before being saved this felt truly devastating. Dare I say I had some thoughts about ending it all because it did cross my mind. Now the way I used to think does not surprise me. I was so engrained in the world's way of thinking that it was all devastating to me.

When you think the way the world does, unconsciously you have been taught it all came together by chance, and that you are nothing more than a cosmic accident, you feel worthless. In the Western world where prayer has been made taboo in many schools, every metric which is deemed bad for society has increased. Suicide rates, murders, teenage pregnancy, violent assaults, you name it, all have increased. Don't believe me? Go and look at the stats for yourself.

I once heard that the word 'darkness' is the word we use to describe the absence of light. Light is constantly moving, darkness does not move. I often hear from sceptics that if God existed why does He allow such evil? In much the same way darkness is merely the absence of light. Evil is the absence of God. It also suggests that these people claim to know what evil is. Have you ever noticed that they accept evil exists? How can they say evil exists if they have not seen good? They all 'borrow' from God's standard. To an unbeliever, evil cannot be defined. In 1936 Adolf Hitler changed the law in Germany to have Jews classified as 'non-persons'. Now under the law, they were not considered as people, and this gave him the ok (at least in his mind) to murder six million of them. I'm sure many Jews questioned their faith during those times.

We do not see the end from the beginning. God does though. When you drive a long distance and you use a Sat Nav for the trip, you might get an idea of an expected time of arrival. Let us say you are taking a 1000-mile drive. You expect to arrive at a certain time. What you don't see are the hurdles you face on the way. You may be in a traffic accident, or one may happen delaying you from getting to your destination. You might have 200 of those miles on the motorway in one go, the Sat Nav only speaks to you when it is time to change course. Once you are on the motorway, it will remain silent for about 190 miles! God's Word is like that. Sometimes we feel like we aren't getting any direction or guidance. Sometimes that simply means you are on the right path for now and to stay there. You can always pray for confirmation of that.

Is Jesus Who He Claims to Be? And can he be trusted?

We must address the question of Jesus Christ himself. A Christian believes that Jesus is God in the flesh and that He came from heaven to pay the price of our sins, as we simply cannot. He then rose again on the third day and defeated death itself.

It is no secret that the Jewish people reject Jesus as the Messiah and that is rooted in religious, historical, and theological differences between Judaism and Christianity. Here are some of the key reasons why they reject him:

Nature of the Messiah: Traditional Jewish expectations of the Messiah differ significantly from the Christian understanding of Jesus. In Judaism, the Messiah is expected to be a human leader descended from King David, who will fulfil specific prophecies and lead the Jewish people in an era of peace, justice, and the full observance of the Torah (Jewish Law and the first five books of the Bible).

Jewish tradition holds the Messiah will bring about a time of universal peace, rebuild the Temple in Jerusalem, gather all Jews back to the Land of Israel, and usher in an era of knowledge of God. Since these conditions were not met during Jesus' lifetime, Jews do not recognise Him as the Messiah. A Christian believes Jesus will do this as part of His Second Coming.

Judaism emphasizes the absolute oneness of God, known as "Shema" (Deuteronomy 6:4). The Christian belief in the Trinity, where Jesus is seen as the Son of God and divine, contradicts Jewish teachings, which reject any division or plurality in God's nature.

The concept of God becoming incarnate in human flesh (Jesus) is foreign to Jewish theology. Jews believe that God is completely transcendent and cannot, or would not, take human form. Muslims also believe that to be the case.

In Judaism, the Messiah is primarily seen as a political and military leader who will redeem the Jewish people from oppression and restore the Davidic kingdom. The idea of a Messiah who suffers and dies for the sins of humanity, as Christians believe, does not align with Jewish expectations.

Christians often interpret passages like Isaiah 53, which speaks of a suffering servant, as referring to Jesus. However, Jewish interpretation generally understands this passage as referring to the suffering of the Jewish people as a collective, or as a righteous individual within the nation, not the Messiah.

During Jesus' lifetime, many Jewish religious leaders did not accept His claims to be the Messiah. This rejection was based on both theological grounds and the perception that Jesus' message and actions did not align with traditional Jewish teachings or expectations of the Messiah.

Because of these, Jews continue to await the coming of the Messiah, who will fulfil all the prophecies in the Hebrew Bible. This ongoing hope for a future Messiah is a central aspect of the Jewish faith. I find it interesting that all religions are waiting for someone...

For Christians, Jesus is considered the Messiah (Christ) based on a combination of scriptural interpretation, theological beliefs, and the events of His life, death, and resurrection. Here are some of the reasons why Christians believe Jesus is the Messiah:

Christians see Jesus' birth in Bethlehem as a fulfilment of Micah 5:2, which speaks of a ruler coming from Bethlehem.

The prophecy in Isaiah 7:14, which speaks of a virgin conceiving a child, is seen by Christians as fulfilled by Jesus.

Isaiah 53 describes a suffering servant who bears the sins of many. Christians see this as a prophecy of Jesus' suffering and crucifixion.

Zechariah 9:9 describes a king coming to Jerusalem on a donkey, which Christians see as fulfilled by Jesus' entry into Jerusalem.

The miracles Jesus performed, such as healing the sick, raising the dead, and casting out demons, are seen as signs of His messianic identity. His teachings, particularly about the Kingdom of God, align with the expectations of the Messiah bringing spiritual and moral renewal.

Jesus spoke with authority, forgave sins, and offered a new understanding of the Law.

Christians believe that His teachings demonstrated His divine authority as the Messiah.

Christians believe that Jesus' death on the cross was the ultimate sacrifice for the sins of humanity, fulfilling the role of the Messiah as one who reconciles humanity with God. This belief is based on passages like Isaiah 53, which speaks of the servant being "pierced for our transgressions."

The resurrection of Jesus is central to Christian belief, that His resurrection was a divine vindication of His identity as the Messiah and a sign of His victory over sin and death. Interestingly, the disciples who ran and denied Him quickly changed their attitude after this event. They all died proclaiming Him to be who He claimed to be. Liars make poor martyrs.

While the Jewish expectation of the Messiah is focused on a political and national deliverer, Christians believe that Jesus' messianic mission was to establish a spiritual kingdom. The kingdom is not of this world but involves the reign of God in their hearts. Christians believe the Second Coming of Christ will be to fulfil the remaining messianic prophecies, such as bringing about universal peace and justice.

The early followers of Jesus, including the apostles, testified to His resurrection and proclaimed Him.

Many scoffers will say; 'Where does Jesus claim to be God?' Jesus does indeed declare himself to be God. Early in my faith journey, I struggled with this. I knew Christians believed Jesus was God and said so but not many knew where and more importantly how. As mentioned in the previous chapter the words used have changed meanings over time. It is worth pointing out that some people will never be satisfied, even if he appears in front of them. Some just do not want to know the truth, all we can do is pray for these people. God can soften the hardest of hearts, including mine! The Bible even says in Matthew 13:58:

58 "And he did not many mighty works there **because of their unbelief.**"

When it comes to the Gospels those who wrote of Jesus give slightly differing views based on their unique perspective, but the important parts are all clear. Let us use an example of what I mean. Let us imagine a car accident. We all go to court to give our evidence of events. What will happen is the driver will give a unique account, the person in the passenger seat will also give a unique account of the event and so would the witness on the street who saw it all happen but was not in the car. Each account would differ, but it would be agreed in court, that the event did in fact happen.

The Bible talks about always having two or more witnesses. The Gospels are written accounts of what they witnessed. A few of the details differ based on their unique perspective but the main event is very clear. They clearly witnessed some unique events in the form of what we would call miracles, and they wrote it all down. What I find interesting is that all the disciples have their doubts, even after witnessing all these events with the most well-known being Peter, denying him three times to sparred being punished with Jesus.

Yet, once Jesus was resurrected after three days, they all saw him and from that point were so sure in their faith in Him that they were all persecuted and killed for their belief in him. Their faith became unshakeable. Peter was even crucified upside down! Post-resurrection is such a huge change in all of them that they went to the grave for it, with the exception being John who survived and was sent to Patmos in Greece where he wrote the book of Revelation. Bad liars do not go to the grave for something they once denied or know is a lie. Liars make poor martyrs. They witnessed something supernatural.

I hear many objections to Jesus even existing, to begin with, but it's worth noting that Jesus does indeed appear outside of the Bible. Many question His existence, despite appearing elsewhere, yet they don't question the existence of Pontius Pilate.

The most notable mentions outside of the Bible are:

Josephus (37-100 AD) who was a Jewish historian who wrote about Jesus in his works, 'Antiquities of the Jews' with two noteworthy passages. The 'Testimonium Flavianum', which mentions Jesus as a wise man and the doer of wonderful works, and the Christ. Another reference to James, "the brother of Jesus, who was called Christ," provides indirect evidence of Jesus' existence.

Tacitus (56-120 AD) was a Roman historian who mentioned Jesus in his annuals referred to Jesus' execution by Pontius Pilate during the reign of Tiberius and mentions the existence of early Christians in Rome.

Pliny the Younger (61-113 AD) was a Roman governor who wrote letters to Emperor Trajan about how to deal with Christians. In his letters, he describes Christians worshipping Christ as God.

Suetonius (69-122 AD) a Roman historian who, in his 'Lives of Caesars', refers to disturbances in Rome caused by "Chrestus," which many scholars believe to be a misspelling of Christ.

Religious Writings:

Talmud: Jewish rabbinical writing that references Jesus in various passages. These passages are often critical but acknowledge His existence and His following.

The Qur'an: Jesus appears in the Muslim book the Qur'an. He is known as Isa in Arabic, but it mentions Him numerous times and recognises Him as a prophet, a messenger of God AND the Messiah, though not the son of God. With key passages including his virgin birth, miracles, and His role in the end times!! Some Muslims, but not all, believe he was the only sinless prophet to walk on this earth. This has always baffled me then why the Muslims would follow the teachings of Muhammad when they have a man here who was virgin born and will return to initiate the latter days while also being sinless. The sticking point for most Muslims tends to be, where is Jesus claiming to be God?

To understand this, we must first see how God reveals himself to Moses in the burning bush in Exodus 3:14:

¹⁴ "And God said unto Moses, **I AM THAT I AM**: and he said, Thus shalt thou say unto the children of Israel, I AM hath sent me unto you."

He introduces himself to Moses as 'I AM', meaning the eternal one and instructs Moses to tell the children of Israel that is who sent you. That is how they will know it is the Lord.

Jesus also introduced himself as 'I AM' in John 8:58:

⁵⁸ "Jesus said unto them, Verily, verily, I say unto you, **Before Abraham was, I am.**"

Once the Jews of the day heard that they wanted to stone Him. They knew what He was claiming. In this passage, Jesus, who is in his 30's at this point, claims to be before Abraham and 'I Am'. The 'I Am' statement meaning eternal. Jesus is claiming to be eternal and before Abraham. It is our modern language that expects him to declare, 'I am God'. In fact, Jesus talks about himself as 'I Am' in these verses:

The light of the world John 8:12:

¹² "Then spake Jesus again unto them, saying, **I am** the light of the world: he that followeth me shall not walk in darkness, but shall have the light of life."

The bread of life in John 6:35:

³⁵ "And Jesus said unto them, **I am** the bread of life: he that cometh to me shall never hunger; and he that believeth on me shall never thirst."

The door in John 10:9:

⁹ "**I am** the door: by me if any man enter in, he shall be saved, and shall go in and out, and find pasture."

The resurrection and life in John 11:25-26:

"Jesus said unto her, **I am** the resurrection, and the life: he that believeth in me, though he were dead, yet shall he live:

And whosoever liveth and believeth in me shall never die. Believest thou this?"

The Way, the Truth and the Life in John 14:6:

⁶ Jesus saith unto him, "**I am** the way, the truth, and the life: no man cometh unto the Father, but by me."

The Vine in John 15:5:

⁵ "**I am** the vine, ye are the branches: He that abideth in me, and I in him, the same bringeth forth much fruit: for without me ye can do nothing."

And finally making references to the Old Testament, He says (I am the God of Moses, Daniel and David, to the point the priest tears his clothes in anger) in Mark 14:62:

⁶² "And Jesus said, **I am**: and ye shall see the Son of man sitting on the right hand of power, and coming in the clouds of heaven."

Then in John 20:28-29, Thomas accepts and calls him my God to which Jesus responds (at last!):

"And Thomas answered and said unto him, **My Lord <u>and my God</u>.**

Jesus saith unto him, Thomas, because thou hast seen me, thou hast believed: blessed are they that have not seen, and yet have believed."

John 10:30-33:

"I and my Father are one.

Then the Jews took up stones again to stone him.

Jesus answered them, Many good works have I shewed you from my Father; for which of those works do ye stone me?

The Jews answered him, saying, For a good work we stone thee not; but for blasphemy; and because that thou, being a man, **makest thyself God."**

Jesus is claiming to have all the traits only applied to God and is the only religious leader who claimed to be God. He also appears in other works besides the Bible acknowledging His existence and post-resurrection. His followers were willing to die for what they had witnessed. For some that will never be enough and that is their decision. But from my studies, there is something very unusual and unique about Jesus of Nazareth and the fact He is still discussed 2000 years later, is something truly special. I don't think we'll be talking about today's celebrities 2000 years from now!

So why wasn't He called Emmanuel?

The name Emmanuel is mentioned in the Bible as a prophetic title rather than a literal name that Jesus would bear. Here's why Jesus was not named Emmanuel.

The prophecy about Emmanuel is found in Isaiah 7:14, which states a virgin shall conceive and bear a son and shall call his name

Emmanuel. The name Emmanuel means 'God with us' in Hebrew, signifying that the coming child would embody God's presence among His people.

The gospel of Matthew references this prophecy, explaining that the birth of Jesus fulfilled the prophecy of Emmanuel. In Matthew 1:23:

²³ "Behold, a virgin shall be with child, and shall bring forth a son, and they shall call his name Emmanuel, which being interpreted is, God with us."

The angel who appeared to Joseph in a dream instructed him to name the child Jesus, which means 'The Lord saves' or 'Yahweh is salvation'.

Jesus was not literally named 'Emmanuel' because 'Emmanuel' serves as a title that describes the nature and mission of Jesus as 'God with us.' The name 'Jesus' was given by divine instruction to emphasize His role as the Saviour. Thus, the prophecy in Isaiah is fulfilled in the person and work of Jesus, who is indeed 'God with us' in His life, death, and resurrection.

Here are some other prophecies concerning Jesus that can be found in the Old Testament:

Malachi 3:1:

"Behold, I will send my messenger, and he shall prepare the way before me: and the Lord, whom ye seek, shall suddenly come to his temple, even the messenger of the covenant, whom ye delight in: behold, he shall come, saith the Lord of hosts."

Psalm 22:1:

1 "**My God, my God, why hast thou forsaken me?** Why art thou so far from helping me, and from the words of my roaring?"

Psalm 22:16:

"For dogs have compassed me: the assembly of the wicked have inclosed me: **they pierced my hands and my feet.**"

Based on many years of study, I concluded that Jesus is indeed who He claims to be. I mean if someone tells me He is God and will be resurrected in 3 days, and then does just that, I'll believe everything He says!

The Holy Trinity

The trinity is often something scoffers will come to. We believe God is one but makes up three persons. However, the word trinity isn't directly used in the scripture. The word Bible isn't used either. You will often see such images as the below:

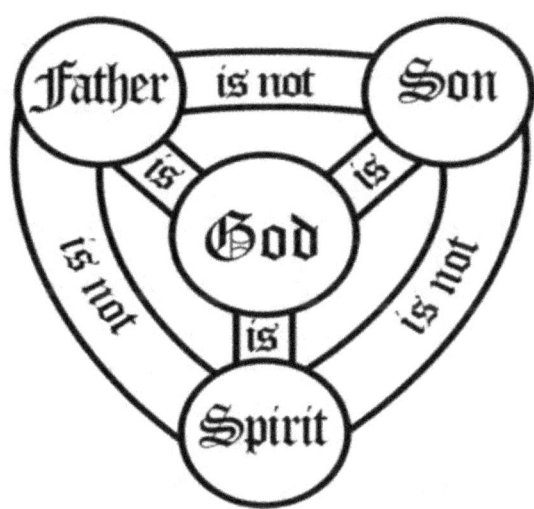

Some will say that 1+1+1= 3. I would argue 1x1x1= 1. A simple explanation is that the human body is a head, torso, legs, and arms. Legs alone do not make the body but are required to form the whole body.

The Bible is 66 separate books. Each book is an individual book, but not the Bible on its own. You draw the same image that Genesis is not the Bible, Matthew is not the Bible, and neither is Revelation, but they all form what is the Bible.

The Trinity doctrine is us attempting to reduce God to a level we can understand. We live in a world of three dimensions. God exists OUTSIDE of our time domain. He is not bound by the same rules and restrictions we are. The fact we cannot fathom how God can be three-in-one, it does not mean it is not possible or even logical. This is seen in geometry and higher levels of space such as a 4-dimensional object, such as a hypercube, otherwise known as tesseract. These objects are mathematically sound. We cannot understand a higher-dimension object as we are bound by three dimensions. The best we have is a 3-D projection of a 4-D object. A 3-D cube is six squares, but ultimately one cube.

Dimensions

If I were to ask you how many degrees were in a triangle?

How many of you said 180 degrees? But what if your triangle was MORE than 180 degrees? What would be your conclusion? Had you made a mistake? In this instance, you have not made a mistake. If you draw out a large triangle on the surface of the earth, you will have more than 180 degrees. This is because there is an additional dimension at play. The curvature of the Earth. See the 180-degree rule is ONLY true in two dimensions. They didn't mention that at school, did they? Most likely your teachers didn't know. When these rules are violated, it can make you question what you have been taught. It should also give you a clue that an additional dimension is present. If you have ever taken a course on Spherical Trigonometry, you will be aware of this rule violation. With a 3D triangle, it is possible to have 90 degrees in all three angles. The rule you learned in school is otherwise known as plain trigonometry. It was this kind of insight that led to the general theory of relativity in 1915.

Some of you may have heard this analogy before. Suppose we have these people called Mr and Mrs. Flat. They have a very distinct handicap. They live in only a two-dimensional space. When he looks at her, he will likely see a line. If I want to reveal myself to them as a three-dimensional being we have some hurdles to overcome. If I placed my finger through their world, they would see a circle or a line. Neither one of them can comprehend what I am because I have the benefit of an extra dimension. When we think of three dimensions we think of height, width, and length. To try and explain three-dimensional objects in two-dimensions:

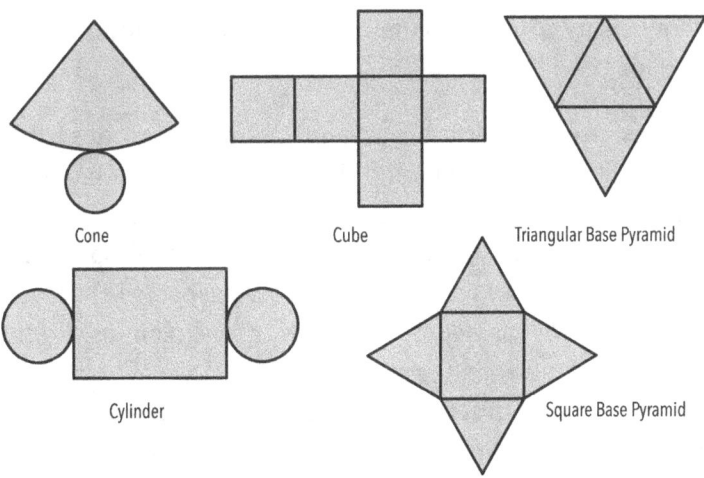

Cone   Cube   Triangular Base Pyramid

Cylinder   Square Base Pyramid

Because we know what these look like in three-dimensional space it is easy to explain. But how to explain a four-dimensional cube? Otherwise known as a tesseract. Now that one is a lot more difficult to explain. Even more so in two dimensions. But as a three-dimensional being, I simply cannot comprehend a four-dimensional object. In his famous painting Corpus Hypercubus painting, Salvador Dali painted the crucifixion of Christ on a four-dimensional cross! Try explaining sounds to someone who was born deaf or colours to someone born blind. It cannot be done. The point here is that we cannot even begin to comprehend God in all his glory and wonder. If we could, He would not be worthy of our worship. This is also why trusting in Him is so important. He can see things we simply cannot.

Ephesians 3:18:

"May be able to comprehend with all saints what is the **breadth**, and **length**, and **depth**, and **height**;

Sorry, how many dimensions is that? Four with one of these being the Greek for time.

Hyperspaces is just a term a mathematician uses to describe more than three dimensions. On June 10th, 1854, a man named Georg Riemann invented Metric Tensors. Einstein then used that mathematics to come up with his four-dimensional spacetime that underpins the theory of relativity. It is now suspected that we live in ten dimensions. We can see the difficulties in explaining a difference with just a one-dimensional change, how could we even comprehend a seven-dimensional difference? If God is a ten-dimensional being, my limited 3D brain cannot even begin to fathom that! But as God seems to like the number seven, if I had to guess I'd go with a seven-dimensional being.

This is one fascinating topic, and certainly one worthy of extra study!

Strength Through Adversity

One of my hobbies happens to be white water rafting. One thing about kayaking in a fast-flowing river is that there are many challenges as you descend the river. Particularly in naturally, uncontrolled rivers! You have eddies that can keep you in one place, and even spin you in circles and will take some effort to get back in the flow. The rocks underneath, many of those unseen, can push you around as they change the current below you, whilst you navigate the waters. Paddling back upstream can be challenging even in slower-moving waters. When the water goes calm though and is easy, it isn't as much fun anymore! It can also be a sign that a drop is coming up. Water goes calm just before a waterfall. Even if I cannot see it yet. The old saying that a smooth sea never made a skilled sailor... The same is true in white water. The same is true in this other river. Times river. If everything is smooth and easy in your life you will not cope well when life starts to get tough. One of Satan's goals over these years is to make our lives easier. People who have it too easy rarely reach out to God, as often as someone who is having a rougher ride, and diamonds are made under great pressure. God has a plan for your life. But to see it you may need to go through a rough river. Sometimes God allows for a little pain in the present to prevent suffering major and enduring pain later. A little bit of Hell will prevent you from going there by repenting of your sin. The pain in your life could well be to remind you that if you continue that trajectory, worse pain is coming. Today's world is lots of pain, but little repentance.

Adversity builds us. Whenever I am having a tough time, and it seems life is getting in the way I will often return to the Book of Job and the story of Joseph. Job was loyal to God. God blessed him and described him as one of the greatest men of the East! (Job 1:3) Then Satan went to God and said he's only loyal to You because You've been so good to him. Notice that Satan had to go to God and ask for permission. He could not just go and wreak havoc on Jobs' life without it.

Job 1:8-22:

⁸ "And the LORD said unto Satan, Hast thou considered my servant Job, that there is none like him in the earth, a perfect and an upright man, one that feareth God, and escheweth evil?

⁹ Then Satan answered the LORD, and said, Doth Job fear God for nought?

Hast not thou made an hedge about him, and about his house, and about all that he hath on every side? thou hast blessed the work of his hands, and his substance is increased in the land.

But put forth thine hand now, and touch all that he hath, and he will curse thee to thy face.

And the LORD said unto Satan, Behold, all that he hath is in thy power; only upon himself put not forth thine hand. So Satan went forth from the presence of the LORD.

And there was a day when his sons and his daughters were eating and drinking wine in their eldest brother's house:

And there came a messenger unto Job, and said, The oxen were plowing, and the asses feeding beside them:

And the Sabeans fell upon them, and took them away; yea, they have slain the servants with the edge of the sword; and I only am escaped alone to tell thee.

While he was yet speaking, there came also another, and said, The fire of God is fallen from heaven, and hath burned up the sheep, and the servants, and consumed them; and I only am escaped alone to tell thee.

While he was yet speaking, there came also another, and said, The Chaldeans made out three bands, and fell upon the camels, and have carried them away, yea, and slain the servants with the edge of the sword; and I only am escaped alone to tell thee.

While he was yet speaking, there came also another, and said, Thy sons and thy daughters were eating and drinking wine in their eldest brother's house:

And, behold, there came a great wind from the wilderness, and smote the four corners of the house, and it fell upon the young men, and they are dead; and I only am escaped alone to tell thee.

Then Job arose, and rent his mantle, and shaved his head, and fell down upon the ground, and worshipped,

And said, Naked came I out of my mother's womb, and naked shall I return thither: **the LORD gave, and the LORD hath taken away; blessed be the name of the LORD.**

In all this Job sinned not, nor charged God foolishly"

Later in Job 2:10:

10 "But he said unto her, Thou speakest as one of the foolish women speaketh. What? shall we receive good at the hand of God, and shall we not receive evil? **In all this did not Job sin with his lips.**"

Job lost everything in a day and through all that Job sinned not. Let that sink in. Job even went so far as to say, 'What God has given, God has taken away'. Do we say that when bad things happen to us? God permitted Satan to TEST Job, but that was not information Job was aware of. Job was completely unaware of the fact God had permitted Satan to make things difficult. He lost everything. His family and servants, his wealth and health. That is a bad day!

In Job 13:15:

15 "Though he slay me, yet will I trust in him:"

The agenda of this book is for you to trust God in all you do with whatever life throws at you. Even when that makes no sense to you at all. When you are doing that, the world will hate you. That will be difficult, Job trusted God. When Job lost everything, he said that what God gave, God took away. That is both trust and faith at work. He understandably got frustrated, and his friends said; 'You must have sinned'. Stay away from 'friends' like this. Like Job, they did not have the full picture. Job was tested and passed. When Job got frustrated, he complained to God in Job 31:35:

35 "Oh that one would hear me! behold, my desire is, that the Almighty would answer me, and that mine adversary had written a book."

God then answered and asked Job 77 rhetorical questions, found in chapters 38-41. Job didn't answer one of them. The questions are meant to highlight God's omnipotence and the limitations of human knowledge and understanding. Some of these questions in Job 38 -39 were:

4 "Where wast thou when I laid the foundations of the earth? declare, if thou hast understanding" (Job 38:4)

Job wasn't there, and God knows that and so did Job. So, what was the point of the question? You parents out there will know that you ask kids questions you already know the answers to, mostly this is to see if your child is being truthful but also for an attitude and reality check!

Job 38:16:

"Hast thou entered into the springs of the sea? or hast thou walked in the search of the depth?"

Scientists didn't know there were springs in the sea until 1977!

Job 38:17-18:

"Have the gates of death been opened unto thee? or hast thou seen the doors of the shadow of death?

Hast thou perceived the breadth of the earth? declare if thou knowest it all."

Job 38:24:

24 "By what way is the light parted, which scattereth the east wind upon the earth?"

Speak to anyone who knows about weather patterns, and they will tell you the light from the sun does indeed cause the wind, by heating the ground and expanding the air thus creating the winds and weather patterns. We can also see light when it is parted through a prism or rainbow. That is just the visible light!

Job 38:35:

35"Canst thou send lightnings, that they may go and say unto thee, Here we are?"

Is this God's way of telling Job electricity can be used to send messages?

These are just a handful of the questions, but you get the point. You can read them all for yourself and attempt to answer them for yourself as if God is asking you now. After all that for Jobs' faithfulness God replenished everything, Job had and more! And your faithfulness will be rewarded as well. If not on the earth, then in heaven.

Job 42:12:

12 "So the LORD blessed the latter end of Job more than his beginning: for he had fourteen thousand sheep, and six thousand camels, and a thousand yoke of oxen, and a thousand she asses."

Another thing we must take note of on the issue of trust is the story of Joseph. His father loved him the most and gave him a coat of many colours, which his brothers hated him for. Many of you will be familiar with the story. Then God gave Joseph dreams which eventually came to pass. He had a dream about his brothers bowing down to him. Joseph was the youngest brother too! But there is something really important so many people overlook.

The dreams showed his future, but they omitted the part where Joseph was sold into slavery, it left out the bit where he had to spend multiple years in prison accused of something he did not do and lied about. Joseph was not given the full picture. God deliberately does not give us the full picture. Why? Think about that. Put the book down and spend time reflecting on why this might be. Then come back.

God doesn't give us the full picture because the journey to our destiny just might intimidate us and as a result, we wouldn't even take the first step. We do not know just how strong we are until strength is our only choice.

Joseph said to his brothers in Genesis 50:20:

[20] "But as for you, ye thought evil against me; but God meant it unto good, to bring to pass, as it is this day, to save much people alive."

What they meant for evil; God meant to use it for good. If Joseph had not endured that, many of the people would have starved. It also meant that his brothers had to come and humble themselves before him. Remember the Bible does NOT say that everything that happens to you will be good. It says it will work together for good for those who love God according to His purpose. His purpose, not ours. Remember the vanilla cake from earlier? When something evil happens to you, wonder what God can use it for later. Think of something bad that happened to you from your past and come up with at least five ways that God can use that for good. For some, this will be tough, but I encourage you to try. Ask the Holy Spirit for help. This exercise is to help shift your thinking.

Romans 8:28:

28 "And we know that all things work together for good to them that love God, to them who are the called according to **his purpose."**

If the Israelites knew there was a Red Sea in the way and 40 years to be spent in the wilderness, they may never have left Egypt. God had Moses led them a longer, less direct route to their destination and omitted the parts that would intimidate them and prevent them from leaving Egypt. God wants our obedience and to put our complete trust in Him. Many of us claim to, but that is simply not so. When Jesus was walking on the water and the disciples were afraid, Peter said, "Lord let me come out on the water". The response from Jesus was: "Come". He did not say, "Come Peter". Of the 12 in that boat, only Peter was willing to put total faith in the Lord, but when he saw what he was doing, doubt crept in, and he started to sink.

Unspeakable Evil

We have all heard of unspeakable evils happening in the world today and I will not claim to know why God allows some of the evils of the world to take place. What I do know however, is that He did stop evil once at the time of the flood. If He were to stop evil right now, He might start with you or me. Funny how we assume everyone else is evil but rarely consider if we are. Have you noticed that those who claim to not believe in God seem to know what evil is? How can they know what evil is if there isn't a standard and lawgiver? If God doesn't exist, then evil is nothing but one person's opinion. The likes of Adolf Hitler, Joseph Stalin, Pol Pot, etcetera didn't technically do evil. If it all came together by chance, how can they even trust their own reasoning? If I could understand God fully, He would not be worthy of my worship.

Job did not understand why his life turned upside down, and neither did Joseph, nor Elijah. God had a higher purpose for them. If we return to our chess example, I'm often willing to sacrifice pieces if it means trapping the King quicker preventing further loss of pieces and ending the game quicker. The pieces removed from the board still exist, they are just no longer in play.

Jesus himself came to this world and experienced first-hand, betrayal, extreme humiliation, and torture. He knows pain. But that had to happen for us to be reconciled to God for without the shedding of blood, there can be no remission of sins. This is mentioned in Leviticus 17:11 and Hebrews 9:22, for the LIFE of the flesh is in the blood. The Jews would make sacrifices for their sins, Jesus who is the Lamb of God, was the final sacrifice. It is why He said, "It is finished", just before He died. The 'debt' had been paid, opening the path directly to God.

We cannot treat people, the way they treat us. Some people really are pure evil and so are the things they do. When people commit evil towards us, how we respond is on us. We cannot treat evil with evil, but by the way Jesus treats you. By doing this we bless our enemies and leave them to the Lord who says, "Vengeance is mine". The Lord tells us to trust him and let Him deal with it. Maybe they'll repent and come to the Lord and be saved, or not. He takes care of us, and He will take care of them too. People may think they are getting away with everything, but in fact, they are storing up God's wrath, which they will experience at full strength should they not repent.

We have all had evils committed against us at some point, some considerably worse than others. Unpopular as it is, we have all committed evils against God too. One of the things the Lord commands is for us to give forgiveness. That is by far one of the hardest things to do, and the worse the offense, the harder it can be to forgive. But forgive we must. We have received radical forgiveness, and we are to give it out, to forgive those who trespass against us. This is one of the most radical Christian beliefs. This doesn't mean we can omit the grieving stage, but forgiving is something we must do. As Jesus says in Matthew 6:11-12 on His famous sermon on the mount:

"For if ye forgive men their trespasses, your heavenly Father will also forgive you:

But if ye forgive not men their trespasses, neither will your Father forgive your trespasses."

I can tell you from first-hand experience that not forgiving others is akin to drinking from a poisoned chalice and will only harm you. It makes you bitter, resentful, and untrusting of others. It was this radical forgiveness of Jesus that made the centurion realise that he really was the Son of God and by giving it out, the world will know beyond any doubt that you too are in Christ.

In one church I went to, the Pastor fell in disgrace. The church had a meeting about it. One question I asked is, once the dust had settled, would he be able to attend church as a member of the congregation? He may not choose to, but would he be welcome, just like all the other sinners in the room? You could tell some were not comfortable with my question. The reality is not one person reading this book is worthy to be in the presence of a Holy God. Jesus did not come to call the righteous, but sinners to repentance. If we stood in front of the congregation and read out all your secret sins, would you leave before we got to your name? I would. You could be sitting next to someone in the church who is truly evil, and not know about it. If we as Christians are not willing to have other sinners come to church, who have had their sins come to the light, then why should God have you in His presence? There is nothing done in the dark that will not come out into the light. Either, in this life or the next.

One of the most, if not the most, famous Christian song is, 'Amazing Grace'. This song was written by a man named John Newton. What most people do not know is that Newton was a slave trader, being a ship captain and investor in the slave trade. In this time he became a slave in West Africa and was subsequently rescued. In 1748 while on board the ship, the Greyhound, a storm caused the ship to sink, and Newton reached out to God and begged for mercy. A few years after his conversion he renounced his former trade and later wrote 'Amazing Grace'. God can give mercy to anyone willing to come to Him in genuine repentance. I do not know why God allowed things like the slave trade to occur but allow it He did.

Here is a thought to consider. In Western nations today most, black communities are more Christian per capita, far more so than their white and Asian counterparts. As we approach the end times mentioned in the Bible, more people are turning away from God. Could God have allowed such things because He will use their descendants to witness for Him as we move closer to the end? If we want our bodies to grow muscle, we must apply resistance to the muscle to force it to grow and become bigger. The more intense the workout, the more progress you see. Some of the strongest believers I know, have experienced the biggest hardships and unknowingly grew their spiritual muscles.

In Due Season

There have been many times in my life when I thought something disastrous happened. Later, when I looked back as a Christian, I realised God was moving me on the next part of my journey. Allow me to share some examples. When I was an Engineering Manager, life was going well. I was paid well, in a job I liked, and had a short commute, so I was able to be home more often. I felt like I was finally succeeding, and I had the job I had been working towards since first going into Engineering.

I had worked my way up from the bottom, as an apprentice. But then I was made redundant, I was given no warning and was just called into the office, told I was no longer required and to get my stuff. I didn't even get the chance to say goodbye to my colleagues and team. On the drive home, I just said, "Lord, I do not understand what or why that just happened, but I trust You that you are leading me to something better and it'll work out just fine and as you intended".

Instead of panicking, I was excited. God's will must have been elsewhere! Instead of being broken, I was delivered. This was the time I was considering selling my possessions so I could meet my financial commitments. I then went to a job, that wasn't that enjoyable or exciting, but it was for a limited time so I could cope with that. It paid better and was even closer than my previous job and allowed me to work from home sometimes. Without that move, this book would not have been possible.

If my life had gone in any other direction at a different time, I may not have come to the Lord at all, or at least much later. God had a plan the whole time. These circumstances are not to derail you but to bring you closer to God's will for your life in due season. He is leading you to something better. If I had stayed with any previous girlfriends, I would not have the wonderful wife and kids I now have. One of the best changes I made in my own life was learning how to tithe and be more generous. I started giving away 10% of my income. When I requested a pay rise, not only did I get it but guess what percentage of pay rise I got? If you said 10%, you'd be right. Sometimes God's will for our life in whatever season isn't always clear but in Hebrews 2:4:

₄ "God also bearing them witness, both with signs and wonders, and with divers miracles, and gifts of the Holy Ghost, according to His own will?"

Sometimes God's will is very obvious, like when a burning bush was talking to Moses. You should pay attention if that happens to you! A dream, a vision, or some other supernatural means. Just keep in mind Satan can do the same.

2 Thessalonians 2:9

₉ "Even him, whose coming is after the working of Satan with all power and signs and lying wonders,"

Satan will use deception. To know we must test the spirits, as some of them will come in the name of Jesus.

1 John 4:1:

₁ "Beloved, believe not every spirit, but try the spirits whether they are of God: because many false prophets are gone out into the world."

2 Corinthians 11:4:

₄ "For if he that cometh preacheth another Jesus, whom we have not preached, or if ye receive another spirit, which ye have not received, or another gospel, which ye have not accepted, ye might well bear with him."

We need to be able to discern the difference. Check the word and ask your Christian pastors to pray for you.

Psalm 37:3-5:

"**Trust in the LORD**, and do good; so shalt thou dwell in the land, and verily thou shalt be fed.

Delight thyself also in the LORD: and **he shall give thee the desires of thine heart.**

Commit thy way unto the LORD; trust also in him; and he shall bring it to pass."

Most of us do not fully trust the Lord to bring it to pass, we try and surpass that bit. Focus on your relationship with Him, you'll get a new heart with new desires. I can personally attest to that.

The Truth

One thing that is apparent in today's society is the phrase, 'your truth'. There is no 'your truth'. There is only the truth. Jesus claims to be the way the truth and the life.

Hebrews 6:18-19

[18] "That by two immutable things, **in which it was impossible for God to lie**, we might have a strong consolation, who have fled for refuge to lay hold upon the hope set before us:

[19] Which hope we have as an anchor of the soul, both sure and stedfast, and which entereth into that within the veil;"

In maths there is only one right answer. Only one answer, thousands of wrong answers. Your truth is a way to get the wrong answer. Truth is that which corresponds with reality. Your truth is a mental health issue. If we don't deal with the truth, you increase mental illness. God is the solution. Every word of God is true. If you love someone, you tell them the truth. Lying to someone, is not loving them, and is NOT Godly, Jesus is where truth begins. Go to the Bible.

John 17:17

17 "Sanctify them through thy truth: thy word is truth."

Matthew 22:16

16 "**And they sent out unto him their disciples with the Herodians, saying, Master, <u>we know</u> that thou art true**, and teachest the way of God in truth, neither carest thou for any man: for thou regardest not the person of men."

Ephesians 4:21

21 "If so be that ye have heard him, and have been taught by him, **as the truth is in Jesus:**"

IF AT ANY POINT YOU DISAGREE WITH THE BIBLE AND ARE NOT FOLLOWING JESUS, YOU ARE THE ERROR. NOT HIM. You are not dealing with reality and will cause yourself harm. When you find something, you don't agree with, you need to be honest with yourself and take it to God first. I don't agree, I am the one who is wrong. You cannot be conformed to this world. YOU CANNOT. If you disagree with the truth, you are the problem, repentance is changing your mind. We can either humbly submit to the word and will of God, or you can argue. Our world is all lies! Do not argue with the author, He is and remains undefeated!

Romans 1:18

¹⁸ "For the wrath of God is revealed from heaven against all ungodliness and unrighteousness of men, **who hold the truth in unrighteousness;**"

This happens EVERY DAY, on social media and news networks.

John 8:32

³² "And **ye shall know** the truth, and the truth shall **make you free**."

If you believe in a lie, you are living in a mental prison and living in a deceptive and demonic rule, pulling hell up, as opposed to going up to heaven. Those who do this are not looking at how to honour the Father. Who is your father? The Father, or the father of lies? I see many people in the churches who have accepted things they should not. We are called to rebuke those not following the faith. We do this BECAUSE we love them. To say nothing and allow them to remain in their sin and believe lies is not loving, telling them the truth is.

The House of Prayer

There is a clear trend within churches today. Many churches are telling people what they want to hear over what they need to hear. However, the primary role of the church is to be the house of prayer. In Matthew 21:13, Jesus declares, "It to be a house of prayer, but you have turned it into a den of thieves". He gets angry and overthrows the tables. Notice He said house of prayer, not of entertainment, games, fashion shows, preaching (although that is required), or even singing and music. We do preach and sing songs of course but its primary function is prayer.

Prayer is its defining activity and there is no substitute for it. The church has drifted from its main calling. The early church was rooted in prayer. They knew the power of it. In Acts 4, after Peter and John had been arrested the response was prayer, during persecution they prayed, and they prayed when choosing the replacement for Judas. We are to go to church to pray and hear the truth. If prayer is not in the church you are in, the Spirit of God will not be present. If you have ever received an answer to prayer, you know first-hand, just how powerful prayer is. Trust Him when He tells you to pray. Prayer is directly talking to God, and if we are ready to listen to Him, He will be willing to speak and that is why it is so important. Fasting is also an important part of our prayer life.

James 5:16

16 "Confess your faults one to another, and pray one for another, that ye may be healed. **The effectual fervent prayer of a righteous man availeth much.**"

And in 1 Timothy 2:8:

8 "I will therefore that men pray everywhere, lifting up holy hands, **without wrath and doubting.**"

Keep A Prayer Journal

It does not matter what happens in your life, there will come a time when doubts come into your mind. Maybe the season you are in is extremely tough. For this reason, it is essential you keep a prayer journal. You have the chance to take part in a supernatural experiment! Whenever you read your Bible and find something you do not understand or need revealing, pray about that and write that down along with the day, date, and time.

You won't get a response immediately, but something will happen to you that will make it clear. A conversation somewhere, a different part of the scripture may reveal it to you, or a dream, to name a few. When that happens, write down what the response was next to the prayer, so you can see where God was active in your life. This way, when times of doubt surface, (and they will) you can return to the journal and see for yourself how God responded to your prayers.

When I first became a Christian, I did not see the point of prayer. God knows the thoughts so what do I need to pray for? God does not need you to pray. The prayer isn't for Him. It is for you. It is something that **you** need, not something He needs. You are not telling God something He didn't know. Prayer is inviting God into your circumstances, bringing revelation for YOU and revealing your heart. Prayer can be silent. God can hear the thoughts. Sometimes praying silently is a good idea as the demonic forces cannot hear it.

God Often Gets The Blame

Have you noticed that when things don't go right, the number of people that blame God for their troubles, instead of looking within at themselves? They fail to see that possibly the reason they are in a predicament is a result of their or someone else's sin.

God often gets the blame for things He did not do. This started in the Garden of Eden. The only instruction in the garden was not to eat from, or touch the tree of The Knowledge of Good and Evil. The serpent here told Eve that she would become, like God, knowing good and evil. Implying that God was withholding something from them, and by obtaining that knowledge they would be like God and ultimately His equal. She did not pause to consider that maybe God withheld that knowledge for a reason.

When Eve did eat and was confronted by God this is how the conversation goes, "...the serpent (that You made) tricked me". Adam then says, "The woman (that you made) got me to eat". You'll notice that there is zero accountability for their actions. It wasn't God's fault they sinned. It was theirs. The real reason the world is in its current state to this day is because of our sins. God did not sin. We did, and still do, and that brings undesired outcomes.

I have wondered what Adam and Eve, but particularly Eve, felt when Cain killed Abel. The Bible doesn't tell us, but I can only imagine the reaction when they truly realised the cost of their sin and disobedience to God's commands. The first murder was between two brothers. One understood God's instructions and one did not. In Genesis 4: 1-4:

1 "And Adam knew Eve his wife; and she conceived, and bare Cain, and said, I have gotten a man from the LORD.

2 And she again bare his brother Abel. And Abel was a keeper of sheep, but Cain was a tiller of the ground.

3 And in process of time it came to pass, that Cain brought of the fruit of the ground an offering unto the LORD.

4 And Abel, he also brought of the firstlings of his flock and of the fat thereof. And the LORD had respect unto Abel and to his offering:"

One thing that God makes clear throughout the scriptures is that the first of all is His.

Leviticus 27:30:

30 "And all the tithe of the land, whether of the seed of the land, or of the fruit of the tree, is the LORD's: it is holy unto the LORD."

In Romans 11:16:

16 "For if the firstfruit be holy, the lump is also holy: and if the root be holy, so are the branches".

Abel brought a sheep, which was the firstlings. Cain brought a fruit. There are two reasons why Abel's offering was accepted. The first is that without the shedding of blood, there can be no remission of sins. Apples do not bleed and are not alive in the biblical classification. Secondly, it was the first of the flock. For Cain it simply says he brought an offering, it didn't say the first of the fruit. The first is the Lords. The plague in Egypt where he took the firstborn sons? The first is His anyway. In Exodus 11:5:

5 "And all the firstborn in the land of Egypt shall die, from the first born of Pharaoh that sitteth upon his throne, even unto the firstborn of the maidservant that is behind the mill; and all the firstborn of beasts."

The first city that Israel took, Jericho, all they took was to be put in the Lord's storehouse. The tithe is the FIRST 10% of what you earn and is to go to the Lord and He'll bless the rest.

So many of us refuse to take responsibility for our actions. God had promised Abram and Sari that they would have a child, even in their advancing years. But Sari got impatient when she couldn't conceive. She did not trust God's timing and tried to force His hand. She then told Abram to 'enter into' her maidservant Hagar. When Hagar got pregnant, she was despised by Sari who then treated Hagar poorly. Ishmael was the result and that is where we get Islam from. Islam came from the birth of an illegitimate child. Right there should be your first warning that Islam is wrong.

God requires a man and a woman to be married. When you do not trust God and His timing you get undesired outcomes. When Hagar left Sari, she was found by an angel of the Lord and Hagar went back. None of that would have been necessary if Abram and Sari had just trusted the Lord to start with! This lack of trust and obedience is also why Adam and Eve were removed from Eden (aka Paradise) because they did not obey God's clear instructions. Today, the state of the world is a direct result of disobeying God's commands.

You cannot serve two masters as mentioned in Matthew 6:24, you'll love the one and hate the other. For most, the world is their master, and they hate God and all those trying to walk in His ways. Instead, choose God. Let Him be your master, have the world hate you instead, it'll pay dividends later. Do you believe that? Do you trust the Lord to deliver you from evil? It's a simple yes or no.

The Crucifixion

God is a just God. He is well within His right to have us all perish. We are all sinners. He is loving and just. **Every sin** must be paid for.

We only need to know two things. Firstly, was Jesus really dead, and second, did He rise from the dead? A lot of people today think of Jesus as a fictional figure such as Zeus, and have little to no research as to whether He existed or not. Even some of the most critical people accept that Jesus did exist and was crucified under Pontius Pilate.

When people think about crucifixion today, they only think about someone being nailed to a cross. However, the nailing of the cross was only one part of it. If you've researched a full Roman crucifixion, you would have a few shocks. What happens first is something called 'flogging or scourging' and would often be called 'the half death', as victims would literally be half dead when it was over. The Romans would use a flagrum (whip) laden with metal and chunks of bone woven in.

This was to remove the flesh at each strike. There are records of people having their veins, arteries, and bones exposed and even their intestines pour out during this process. The Jews had laws that wouldn't allow for more than 40 whips. Because of this they would have someone else keep count and would often stop at 39 just in case of a miscount. The Romans would deliberately ignore this Jewish law, so it is likely Jesus had more than 40 lashes. This was designed to remove flesh painfully. Jesus then had to carry his own cross in this state!

The next part was to nail them to the cross. When most people think of the hand where Jesus had the nails they often point to the palm. This is not correct. In those days the hand was considered from the wrist down. They put the nail in what we today would consider the wrist. The reason for this is because the nerve that makes you uncomfortable every time you hit it, or the 'funny' bone' is that nerve. Now imagine having a nine-inch nail being driven through your 'funny' bone nerve.... Makes me cringe whenever I think of it! The positioning of the nails in the feet was also deliberate as it meant that to even breathe, those hanging there had to push off of the nail with their feet just to be able to breathe. That is why the Romans then broke their legs so they could no longer push upward and would slowly suffocate. Nobody survived a Roman crucifixion. It was designed to be one of the most painful and humiliating ways to die. In the case of Jesus, they also pieced his side. This fits the scripture; "They shall look upon me, whom they pierced."- Zechariah 12:10.

There are records of Jesus' crucifixion. We have the four Gospels of Matthew, Mark, Luke, and John.

The other mentions are in Josephus, Tacitus, and Mara Bar-Serapion, a Syrian philosopher who wrote a letter to his son sometime after 73 AD. In the letter, he refers to the execution of a 'wise king' of the Jews, which many interpret to be Jesus. The crucifixion is also a practice well documented in history. It is also fair to say that Jesus was indeed crucified under Pilate.

The resurrection is one of the central tenets of Christianity. For many historians, this topic remains of interest and debate. Most of the accounts are within the Gospels, in 1 Corinthians 15:3-8, Jesus was seen by over 500, and all the Gospels agree the tomb was empty. For me the sheer boldness of the early Christians who went to the grave for this, I do not know anyone who would do that for a lie. Do you?

Saved Versus Unsaved

There are only two kinds of people in the world. Saved and unsaved. God isn't willing that any should perish but all come to repentance (2 Peter 3:9). There is an invisible barrier everywhere you go for those who are saved, and those who are not. When was the last time you spoke to someone about your faith and tried to win them to Christ? If we just spoke to one person a week that would be 52 people in a year, we could have planted seeds for the Lord. What if you spoke to one person a day? That would be 365 people possibly won over to the Lord. Many do not share their faith. Is it because they feel the pressure of the world? Is it because they do not have the confidence to provide at least some of the answers? When I started on my faith journey this was a big stumbling block for many Christians.

Jesus often spoke about the separation in parables.

Matthew 25:32-33:

"And before him shall be gathered all nations: and **he shall separate them one from another, as a shepherd divideth his sheep from the goats:**

And he shall set the sheep on his right hand, but the goats on the left."

The weeds among the wheat in Matthew 13:24-30:

"Another parable put he forth unto them, saying, The kingdom of heaven is likened unto a man which sowed good seed in his field:

But while men slept, his enemy came and sowed tares among the wheat, and went his way.

But when the blade was sprung up, and brought forth fruit, then appeared the tares also.

So the servants of the householder came and said unto him, Sir, didst not thou sow good seed in thy field? from whence then hath it tares?

He said unto them, An enemy hath done this. The servants said unto him, Wilt thou then that we go and gather them up?

But he said, Nay; lest while ye gather up the tares, ye root up also the wheat with them.

Let both grow together until the harvest: and in the time of harvest I will say to the reapers, Gather ye together first the

tares, and bind them in bundles to burn them: but gather the wheat into my barn."

Is Jesus talking about hell here when he refers to bind them in bundles to burn them? I think so.

The two sons in Matthew 21:28-32:

"But what think ye? A certain man had two sons; and he came to the first, and said, Son, go work to day in my vineyard.

He answered and said, I will not: but afterward he repented, and went.

And he came to the second, and said likewise. And he answered and said, I go, sir: and went not.

Whether of them twain did the will of his father? They say unto him, The first. Jesus saith unto them, Verily I say unto you, That the publicans and the harlots go into the kingdom of God before you.

For John came unto you in the way of righteousness, and ye believed him not: but the publicans and the harlots believed him: and ye, when ye had seen it, repented not afterward, that ye might believe him."

The ten virgins in Matthew 25: 1- 13:

[1]"Then shall the kingdom of heaven be likened unto ten virgins, which took their lamps, and went forth to meet the bridegroom.

And five of them were wise, and five were foolish.

They that were foolish took their lamps, and took no oil with them:

But the wise took oil in their vessels with their lamps.

While the bridegroom tarried, they all slumbered and slept.

And at midnight there was a cry made, Behold, the bridegroom cometh; go ye out to meet him.

Then all those virgins arose, and trimmed their lamps.

And the foolish said unto the wise, Give us of your oil; for our lamps are gone out.

But the wise answered, saying, Not so; lest there be not enough for us and you: but go ye rather to them that sell, and buy for yourselves.

And while they went to buy, the bridegroom came; and they that were ready went in with him to the marriage: and the door was shut.

Afterward came also the other virgins, saying, Lord, Lord, open to us.

But he answered and said, Verily I say unto you, I know you not.

Watch therefore, for ye know neither the day nor the hour wherein the Son of man cometh."

The door was shut. In the parable of the ten virgins, these women represent Christians! All looked ready, maybe even walked the walk, but they were empty of the Spirit and were not prepared. The lamp did not light their way. The oil did. That is something that cannot be shared. Many think they are prepared but they are not, and it represents an irreversible loss. The oil represents the Holy Spirit, it is why the oil could not be shared in the story. We are to live in faithful readiness. The door being shut is found at Noah's Ark, the five foolish virgins, and the narrow door. It symbolises a final closure. There is no hint in scripture that once that door is closed, it can be reopened.

I believe this is also pointing for us to remain watchful as we do not know the time the Lord will return. But once the door is eventually shut. It will be shut forever. God is love, mercy, and graceful. But these will have an expiry date and at some point, judgement will follow. God gave the people a 120-year warning before sending the flood. Jesus speaks about separation often. The parables highlight a final separation of those saved and those who are not.

Where you sit at work, when you go to the gym, at a family event, or even in your church, there is an invisible dividing line separating the two groups. At some point, the saved and unsaved will be separated into two distinct groups. Those that will go with Him and those that will not. What side will you be on? Can you confidently and boldly say you will be going with Him? For me the scariest verses in the whole Bible are found in Matthew 7:22-23:

"Not every one that saith unto me, Lord, Lord, shall enter into the kingdom of heaven; but he that doeth the will of my Father which is in heaven.

Many will say to me in that day, Lord, Lord, have we not prophesied in thy name? and in thy name have cast out devils? and in thy name done many wonderful works?

And then will **I** profess unto them, **I never knew you: depart from me**, ye that work iniquity."

There are some in the church who cast out devils in the name of Jesus and will NOT see the Kingdom of heaven. They do many wonderful works in the name of Jesus but are far from Him in their hearts because they have gone the way of the world. The word of God is the polar opposite to what the world teaches. There are many things that Christians should not accept because the Lord himself does not accept them. The issue of marriage is one such thing.

A marriage is between one man and one woman only. Marriage is a covenant between a man and a woman becoming one, declaring their vows and commitment to God. God only made one wife for Adam. Anything other than that is known as sexual immorality. If people only had a partner at marriage, how many sexually transmitted diseases would there be? Like none. Because we were made pure and would have stayed that way. It is our own lusts and desires that have brought about unwanted consequences of STDs, such as AIDs and HIV. It wasn't God's fault. It was ours. The scriptures are clear on what is acceptable and what is not. Too many people want to ignore God's clear commands to do what their heart desires and do what is right in their own eyes. Jesus warns us about this attitude in Revelation 3:16:

16 "So then because thou art lukewarm, and neither cold nor hot, I will spue thee out of my mouth."

Jesus is warning us about being lukewarm. We cannot afford to bend the scriptures to what modern society deems acceptable. What society deems acceptable, God does not. He gives a dire warning to those going against His clear instructions. Do not follow the world, friendship with the world is enmity with God. For those who are doing these wicked things, we should be praying for them, love and care for them but under no circumstances tell them their sin is ok and endorse it.

There are six things the Lord hates. These are found in Proverbs 6:16-19:

"These six things doth the LORD hate: yea, seven are an abomination unto him:

A proud look, a lying tongue, and hands that shed innocent blood,"

¹⁸ "An heart that deviseth wicked imaginations, feet that be swift in running to mischief,"

¹⁹ "A false witness that speaketh lies, and he that soweth discord among brethren."

Lying is mentioned twice. We have all lied at some point. Hands that shed innocent blood…. That includes abortion. The heartbeat starts at three weeks and one day. I hear many excuses for why abortion is ok. It isn't, it is murder pure and simple. Have you ever noticed that if a baby is aborted it is considered a fetus but if that expectant mother is murdered, they say the woman and her 'unborn child' were murdered? This is because you can get a longer sentence for a double murder. It is an unborn child when it suits! We all know it is an unborn child. People are trying to justify their own wickedness. Once you have truly been born again the Holy Spirit will convict you. If you are ok with a lot of these issues, then put simply you are what Jesus calls lukewarm. Remember if the world loves you, then you are not as close to the Lord as you think you are. The world hated Jesus and it should hate you too.

I see many Christians who profess Christ yet take their children to Halloween parties. If that is you, can I humbly ask you to reconsider what you are doing? Celebrating Halloween as a Christian is like the Jews celebrating the holocaust! We are not meant to celebrate death and witchcraft. The Bible warns heavily against this. It describes death as an enemy in 1 Corinthians 15:26. You are inviting all kinds of wicked spirits into your heart and your life. Don't do it. You'll thank me later. Keep your eyes, the windows to your soul guarded at ALL times.

There are plenty of people who believe in God but are not saved. In James 2:19:

[19] "Thou believest that there is one God; thou doest well: **the devils also believe, and tremble.**"

The devils believe. They are not saved. People who are not saved include unbelievers, who think the Gospel is foolish. A category I was once in with others who do not confess Christ with their mouth or believe it in their heart that He rose from the dead. Confessing Christ with your mouth is the easy part, anyone can do that. The hard part comes from believing it in your heart that He rose from the dead. If you believe those things your behaviour should reflect that. Once the Holy Spirit truly dwells within you, you are repentant of the sins you have committed. The Gospel is veiled to them because it goes against the wisdom of this world, and they wish to continue in their sin. It is only veiled to those who are perishing as read in 1 Corinthians 1:18:

[18] "For the preaching of the cross is to them that perish foolishness; but unto us which are saved it is the power of God."

The goal of this book is to give you some knowledge and answers to the questions. Other parts will be left open for you to go and discover for yourself. But from God's perspective, you are either in the body of Christ or you are not. It really boils down to two things. We read in Romans 10:9:

⁹ "That if thou shalt confess with thy mouth the Lord Jesus, and shalt believe in thine heart that God hath raised him from the dead, thou shalt be saved."

Is it really that simple? Well, yes actually. Believing Jesus is Lord is the first part and then confessing it openly, but do you also believe it in your heart that He was raised from the dead? Why would so many fall away if they truly believed? In 2 Thessalonians 2:3:

³ "Let no man deceive you by any means: for that day shall not come, except there come a **falling away** first, and that man of sin be revealed, the son of perdition"

The word rapture isn't used anywhere in the Bible, but it refers to when God comes to claim his people. I think many Christians believe millions of people will vanish in an instant. While that could be possible, I am not so convinced. I do not know how many people were around when Noah built the Ark. But for simplicity let us say 250,000. Anyone could have gone onto the Ark. God gave plenty of warning! But how many were saved from the flood? Only eight. EIGHT. Many of Noah's own family did not survive the flood. The world had become corrupt and filled with violence. Anyone could have gone on the Ark, but many refused. On October 7th 2023 a terrorist group called Hamas invaded Israel, taking several hostages. The word violence in the Hebrew is 'Hamas'. In the days of Noah, the world was filled with...violence (Hamas).

If millions are to be saved why would Jesus say in Luke 18:8:

⁸ "I tell you that he will avenge them speedily. Nevertheless when the Son of man cometh, shall he **find faith on the earth?**"

Why would Jesus ask such a question? This isn't clear whether this is before the rapture of the church or after, but faith is going to be rare when the Lord returns.

If you are one of those people who believes but does not share your faith at all, then there are only really three conclusions as to why you don't share it:

You don't really believe it.

You cannot justify why you believe it as you haven't given much thought to it.

You do not care if others are going to hell.

Now I know that is direct. The truth hurts and upsets people. It is why so many are offended just at the mention of Jesus Christ. Because it stirs their sinful desires. As Christians, we believe that Jesus is God in the flesh and the only way to Heaven is through him. If you love the people around you, share your faith with the knowledge and confidence, being ready to provide an answer to all those who seek a reason to believe. If they choose to reject it, that is on them.

You however must plant the seeds and pray to the Lord that he will open their eyes to see and ears to hear. But by sharing your faith, you have done what you can to bring them to the truth and the Lord, the rest is up to them to open their heart. You must keep your eye on eternity. If you love these people, wouldn't you want to see them in Heaven? This life on Earth is just a fleeting moment. We are called to be disciples to preach to all nations. We are not called just to attend church each week and then go about our week like everyone else. The people would have laughed at Noah. I'm sure they weren't laughing when the flood waters came. You must be bold as a Christian and be steadfast in the faith.

Enter in at the narrow gate... In Matthew 7:13-14:

13 "Enter ye in at the strait gate: for wide is the gate, and broad is the way, that leadeth to destruction, and many there be which go in there at:

14 Because strait is the gate, and narrow is the way, which leadeth unto life, and few there be that find it."

The sad reality is that the vast majority **will not go** into the Kingdom of Heaven. Many will fall away, some will outright reject it, giving heed to seducing spirits and some just don't want it. The path to life is narrow. Broad is the way that leads to destruction. How many people have lived since Jesus departed? Most of those were not on the narrow path.

More people are on the path to Hell than to Heaven. Do not be one of those who use the wide gate. It is also worth noting that when Jesus speaks this, He is doing so in the presence of believers. People who claim to know God. Just because people profess, they are Christian, it does not mean they are one. When a lot of foreign nationals, particularly from Eastern cultures, come to the Western countries that claim to be Christian, they see all the immorality going on in the society and impute that onto Christianity. In reality, many Western nations haven't been Christian for some time.

The world will say that Jesus loves you, and you will be saved. However, you cannot force someone to love you. It must be two ways. If you do really love someone and they do not feel the same way, you must let them go. Jesus will not force Himself onto anyone who does not want him.

You must be born again. Your old behaviours must go, do not let anybody tell you that you are, ok as you are and just be you. There are 1000 ways and gates to Hell, but only one to Heaven. Choose the narrow path. Consciously staying on the Lord's path requires effort. There are many things we should not do, not only as Christians but anyone. We all instinctively know it is wrong to murder, to lie, and to commit adultery. Some people are good at suppressing that, but their heart lets them know that what they are doing is wrong.

In Romans 2:15:

15"Which shew the work of **the law written in their hearts**, their conscience also bearing witness, and their thoughts the mean while accusing or else excusing one another,"

God's law is written on every heart of every person. When the flood happened there was no printed Bible. God expected them to know the law, He had written it on their hearts.

Humility will take us a long way with God. Jesus warned against self-righteousness in the parable of the Pharisee and tax collector. The Pharisee went prideful to God while the tax collector went humbly. The scripture tells us that God resists the proud but gives grace to the humble. The tax collector went home justified before God. Once we are saved, we need to be careful not to get self-righteous and act humbly toward others.

You must trust Jesus for your salvation and nobody else, including yourself.

John 11:26:

26 "And whosoever liveth and believeth in me shall never die. Believest thou this?"

It's also important to know that God understands our thoughts, our darkest thoughts, and the thoughts which have a genuine desire to know Him. Our thoughts are vanity. We may go to the gym because we want a better body and a healthier lifestyle. Or we may go buy a bigger house or a nicer car trying to keep up with the Joneses. If God has blessed you with a better-paying job, it isn't for us to live more lavishly and buy that bigger house. It is for us to give more generously. If God has blessed you financially, give more generously. God will meet your needs. Remember our needs and our wants are NOT the same thing.

In Chronicles 28:9:

9 "And thou, Solomon my son, know thou the God of thy father, and serve him with a perfect heart and with a willing mind: **for the LORD searcheth all hearts, and understandeth all the imaginations of the thoughts: if thou seek him, he will be found of thee**; but if thou forsake him, he will cast thee off forever."

He understands the imagination of the thoughts!

In Psalm 94:11:

11 "The LORD knoweth the thoughts of man, that they are vanity."

It also says in Luke 11:17, that Jesus, knew their thoughts. There is a clue in His divinity right there.

God knows the reasons why we do the things we do. Are you doing something to look good in front of your fellow man and/or congregation or are you doing it to please the Lord? Whatever it is you do, do it for an audience of one.

Fake Christians

Just because someone says they are Christian, it doesn't mean they are. Sadly, there are now many fake Christians who are really anti-Christ. They accept worldly pursuits and thus become more worldly. Accepting things, they should not and is clearly against the scriptures.

Corinthians 11:3-4:

[3] "But I fear, lest by any means, as the serpent beguiled Eve through his subtilty, so your minds should be corrupted from the simplicity that is in Christ.

[4] For if he that cometh preacheth another Jesus, whom we have not preached, or if ye receive another spirit, which ye have not received, or another gospel, which ye have not accepted, ye might well bear with him."

2 Corinthians 11: 13-14

[13] "For such are false apostles, deceitful workers, transforming themselves into the apostles of Christ.

11 And no marvel; for Satan himself is transformed into an angel of light."

Satan disguises himself as an angel of light, and so do his followers and we must push against this evil agenda and not accept it. It should not be a surprise though. The fake Christians however, have infiltrated the church, taking leadership positions while trying to 'modernise' it.

4 "For there are certain men crept in unawares, who were before of old ordained to this condemnation, ungodly men, turning the grace of our God into lasciviousness, and denying the only Lord God, and our Lord Jesus Christ." (Jude 4)

Fake Christians invade, they want to get into the churches and into leadership and teach false doctrines as predicted. They pretend to be on Team Jesus when they are Team Satan. These people accept gay marriage and adulterous behaviour when the scripture teaches against it. It is a trojan horse and People accept inviting in this ideology and demonic force into your boundary is highly dangerous. They have invaded God's house. Satan was with God and tried to overthrow the house of God from within. He did it in heaven and was cast out. He did it in the garden, he did it again with Judas, and the tactic has not changed. The biggest threat to the church is not those on the outside, but those who have invaded from within. By doing so, he is leading people straight to hell.

The upcoming generation is so broken because they have been told there are more than two genders, you can live how you want, have sex with whom you want, and with as many partners as you want. God, however, put some rules down to ensure we do not completely destroy ourselves. A fireplace in the home is warm and cosy, but only when contained to the fireplace. If you let it spread, it will burn your entire house down. We are currently living in a world where there is no sexual boundary, and it has become perverse because the real Christians did not put a stop to it and allowed that evil to grow and flourish. The flames of passion are to be contained within the boundary of marriage. Satan is trying to move God's line until there is no line at all.

God made us male and female, little Jimmy claims he's a girl and wants to go to the female locker room, NO! These people also push non-monogamy instead of just saying perverts. They are also attempting to push the age of consent as to not demonise those who sexualize children. Because they do not want any limitations. There is even a Californian Senate Bill 145 stating that child perverts do not need to register as sex offenders if the victim is 14 years old or older, and if the offender is no more than 10 years older than the victim. If a 24-year-old has sexual relations with a 14-year-old, they do not have to register as sex offenders and can then potentially go and get a job in a school. The real Christians need to hold the line and say NO! We have done a poor job of that in recent years.

There is no salvation for them unless; we follow Jude 22-23:

22 "And of some have compassion, making a difference:

23 **And others save with fear, pulling them out of the fire**; hating even the garment spotted by the flesh."

It is the responsibility of real Christians to do our utmost to pull them out of the fire so they can come to the Lord who can save them. Everything in life pulls us into decline, we need to work hard on all aspects of our life. Unless we are working on something, it will eventually fall into decline. This is true with our spiritual health too.

There is a constant demonic force trying to pull us down when we should be aiming and reaching upward. When someone tells you, to just wait things will get better. Nope. Jude 3:

³ "Beloved, when I gave all diligence to write unto you of the common salvation, it was needful for me to write unto you, **and exhort you that ye should earnestly contend for the faith** which was once delivered unto the saints."

The word contend means to deal with something, state, assert, or complete. We must address the Christians who say they are following Jesus, yet their actions are no different from those of the world. God calls you beloved. Our relationship with the one true God is what defines us as a people.

There are many ways to come to the knowledge of the truth in Jesus and I enjoy hearing the stories. There is only ONE way to the Father though and that is through Jesus and if you love Him, keep the commandments. There is ONE door to heaven, and that door is narrow. Make EVERY EFFORT to go through that narrow door. Those that are truly in Jesus, are willing to die, suffer, fight, and lose their job for Him because He matters to them. The fake Christians accept Jesus as saviour but not as Lord and Master and do not want Him to rule over them. If he doesn't though, Satan will. They want God's forgiveness but not His leadership. The world prefers fake Christians, and we need to say NO to them and not be ashamed of the Gospel of Jesus and push back. Remember Biblical Christianity is unpopular.

Satan is the master deceiver. He disguises himself as an angel of light! All the movies of him as a red devil are just plain wrong. He will come across as a good guy. He has even been glorified in shows like Lucifer. Even his ministers will appear righteous. We can see the tactics in society now, where the temperature of the world is being turned up.

I am reminded of the story in Daniel, where the Jews were required to bow to the image of Nebuchadnezzar. But Shadrach, Meshach, and Abednego refused. The King then commanded the men to be put into a furnace. The three friends were then cast in, this time the Lord protected them. The friends had two choices, go with the world or go with God. They made the right choice. Even if God had not delivered them in the furnace, for the three friends, that furnace was the closest to hell they would ever be and was only for a fleeting moment. They were being purified.

For Nebuchadnezzar, however, that will be the closest to heaven he would get and had a permanent furnace waiting for him in hell. This same spirit also worked through Adolf Hitler, when they were having some trouble with the Jews, they put them in a furnace! Different times and people but the spirit of the Anti-Christ remains the same. At some point, the world will turn the pressure up so much that many Christians and non-Christians will bow to worship the image of the Anti-Christ. As Christians however, we must resist this at all costs. We will experience great turmoil for rebelling against the Anti-Christ, but we must keep our focus on eternity and not just a fleeting moment in time.

The people accepting some of these worldly things have been deceived into believing they are okay and approved by God. Jesus gives a warning about this attitude in Revelation 3:15-21:

"I know thy works, that thou art neither cold nor hot: I would thou wert cold or hot.

So then because thou art lukewarm, and neither cold nor hot, I will spue thee out of my mouth.

Because thou sayest, I am rich, and increased with goods, and have need of nothing; and knowest not that thou art wretched, and miserable, and poor, and blind, and naked:

I counsel thee to buy of me gold tried in the fire, that thou mayest be rich; and white raiment, that thou mayest be clothed, and that the shame of thy nakedness do not appear; and anoint thine eyes with eyesalve, that thou mayest see.

As many as I love, I rebuke and chasten: be zealous therefore, and repent.

Behold, I stand at the door, and knock: if any man hear my voice, and open the door, I will come in to him, and will sup with him, and he with me.

To him that overcometh will I grant to sit with me in my throne, even as I also overcame, and am set down with my Father in his throne."

We cannot afford to be lukewarm Christians and must overcome the trials and temptations of the world. If our worldview doesn't upset the world, we are doing something wrong. Jesus still loves you, but you will be rebuked and still need to repent. In these verses, Jesus is talking about Christians having one foot in the Word and the other in the world. In His words, He will spue (vomit/spit) you out of His mouth. Jesus offers salvation, to anyone willing to listen. If you are a lukewarm Christian, take your faith seriously and do not be like the five virgins caught unprepared.

John 14:6:

⁶ "Jesus saith unto him, I am the way, the truth, and the life: **no man cometh unto the Father, but by me."**

John 14:15:

¹⁵ **"If ye love me, keep my commandments."**

In Matthew 15:8-9:

"This people draweth nigh unto me with their mouth, and honoureth me with their lips; but their heart is far from me.

<u>**But in vain they do worship me, teaching for doctrines the commandments of men.**</u>"

If we love the Lord we must obey the commandments, this includes some of the more obscure commands mentioned in previous chapters, not just the ten! Jesus is saying the lukewarm Christians honour Him with their lips, but have their hearts far from him. Their efforts will be in vain. The lukewarm crowd, those ok with what the Bible clearly teaches against, will be hearing this from Matthew 7:21-23:

"Not every one that saith unto me, Lord, Lord, shall enter into the kingdom of heaven; but he that doeth the will of my Father which is in heaven.

Many will say to me in that day, Lord, Lord, have we not prophesied in thy name? and in thy name have cast out devils? and in thy name done many wonderful works?

And then will I profess unto them, I never knew you: depart from me, ye that work iniquity."

If this statement doesn't concern you, it should. Most Christians do not cast out devils, some Christians won't even talk about devils and possession anymore! Even people who have cast out devils and prophesied in His name will be rejected because they will do things openly while doing something different in private. It is entirely possible to have a head knowledge of Christ yet miss the heart knowledge. The devils believe and tremble, but they are not saved though.

Chapter 3
What You Believe Is Limited By What You Know

Your Worldview

What is your worldview? Do you think it matters? Many do not entertain this very question. But our worldview determines how we behave, how we treat others, what we deem acceptable, and our hopes and aspirations for the future. Your worldview starts to take shape the moment you are born. Everything we do stems from it. It matters a lot. Take the time to think of your answers to the following questions:

Who am I?
What am I worth?
Where did I come from?
Why am I here?
Where am I going when I die?

Once you have asked yourself these questions, ask yourself where your worldview came from. There are generally two major worldviews. One is based on evolution where we evolved from bacteria, which in turn somehow came from non-living material (yes really) over millions of years. The other based is on creation. These two worldviews could not be more different and as a former atheist, when I asked myself these questions the answers were striking. Who am I and what am I worth? Well, if evolution was true then I'm nobody important, I just appeared throughout millions of years, with an explosion from nothing.

Think about just how much faith that belief requires. It would mean I am an accident and ultimately, I'm worth nothing, and neither is anybody else. In turn, it means that life is just a by-product of other natural processes so if I want to do something I can just do it right? Steal from you, beat or even kill you if I don't like you? Take away your child and put them in a gas chamber? The purpose of life is to preserve yourself and pass on your genes, survival of the fittest! But is it? If a whale swims through a school of fish, it is no longer survival of the fittest. It becomes the survival of the luckiest. When I die, I'll just go back to being compost and get recycled into something else. No consequences, no problem.

But what if there was a creator? A God who sees all things. The answers to these five questions become radically different. Who am I? What is my purpose? What gifts do I have? Every person has unique gifts, and every person is unique. Rare things are valuable! It's the reason antiques reach high prices! I've yet to meet anyone who doesn't have a special talent for something. Those labelled stupid or 'dunces' by their peers are simply not taking the time to find the uniqueness within each individual. When I was at school there were some subjects, I simply could not stand, my attention wanned, and I was not pleased to be there. As a child, you cannot just say 'no' to something that does not interest you. As a result, many people go through life without ever discovering their own uniqueness given to them by their creator.

Psalm 139:14 states:

[14] "I will praise thee; for I am fearfully and wonderfully made...."

And Jeremiah 1:5:

⁵ "Before I formed thee in the belly I knew thee; and before thou camest forth out of the womb I sanctified thee,..."

If that is true then I was specifically made and one of a kind. Rare things are unique and of value, which is why antiques reach such high prices! The purpose of life?

Colossians 1:16:

¹⁶ "For by him were all things created, that are in heaven, and that are in earth, visible and invisible, whether they be thrones, or dominions, or principalities, or powers: **all things were created by him, and for him**"

Where did I come from? Well according to the Bible, I was formed from the dust of the ground. It's interesting then that everything found in the ground is also found in you. The human body contains four to five grams of IRON. Without it you would be dead, we have all met someone who is iron deficient. Five grams isn't much but is essential to your survival! You are finely tuned.

When I die, I am going back to dust and my spirit to be with the Lord, where I can be what we were originally meant to be prior to the fall. Raised incorruptible.

Why am I here? We all have unique gifts. How do we use those gifts?

Those two worldviews could not be more different. If you look closer, the evolution worldview is the opposite of God's. More on this in a bit. These two worldviews are no more than two opposing religions. Faith is required to believe both, but creation has more evidence in its favour than is taught in the school system. In my opinion, both views with competing evidence should be presented, only then can you think critically and form a more rounded view.

But what even creates your worldview? It starts when you enter this world. Your parents will pass off their views to you, whether they mean to or not. All through school, I was taught I evolved from millions of years of evolution and have common ancestry with every other animal. Is it any wonder then why so many people today, behave like animals? As a child, you just believe everything you are told and rarely, if ever, question that. Despite the fact that the knowledge you obtain on your journey may suggest something different. You can lead a human to knowledge, but you can't make it think.

What you believe determines how you behave. If you believe that there is a creator who sees all things, you are more likely to watch how you behave, act, treat others, and expose yourself to. There is a reason there are so many cameras in our towns and cities. People behave differently when they know they are being watched. People have often said to me that the idea of God came about by men and kings to keep the people in check. An argument I once bought into and even used myself in debates.

But with study and research, I started to see that the idea of a divine creator wasn't so foolish after all. I started to look a little deeper with a genuine interest to understand. For me, it all changed when I took a job in engineering, and I use engineering examples in this book, however, I discovered very quickly that even something as basic as a screwdriver does not simply come into existence by chance over millennia on its own. Take a look around your home. Every item you see first had to be an idea in somebody's mind! From the carpet to the wall, the kettle, etcetera. What makes people believe then that nature, in all its complexity, came about by chance? Do you need to see the person who assembled your phone to know they exist?

The whole theory of evolution is based on death and rebirth. To get a better more advanced species what must happen to the 'lesser' versions? They must die. Otherwise, the lesser genes risk being mixed in with the more advanced gene pool. This was the thinking behind the Nazi Germany regime. The 'pure' race, blonde hair, blue eyes, etcetera. There are a lot of propaganda photos of Adolf Hitler outside churches, but he was about as Christian as Satan.

Proverbs 8:36:

36 "But he that sinneth against me wrongeth his own soul: **all they that hate me love death.**"

The Bible teaches that death is an enemy in 1 Corinthians 15:26:

26 **"The last enemy that shall be destroyed is death."**

Hitler believed the Germans were the superior species and in 1936 classified the Jews as 'Nonpersons'. Now under German law, the Jews were no longer considered people which is what gave him an okay in his mind to kill 6 million of them. They were just animals that breed like vermin, no different from rats. The Japanese treated the American soldiers like animals for a similar reason. They conducted several studies to suggest they were the most evolved because they had less body hair than the Americans and thus the Americans were closer to animals. This thinking shouldn't be too much of a surprise if you believe you evolved from nothing and are a higher species of animal.

In fact, Adolf Hitler is quoted as saying:

"People will believe a big lie over a small one."

"Tell the lie long enough, loud enough and often enough and the people will believe it."

The theory of evolution is a big lie that has been shouted so loud and for so long that people now just believe it without spending too much time studying it, and looking into the counter-evidence, as it may crush their worldview and bring them to the truth.

In 1859 Charles Darwin famously wrote a book called, 'The Origin of Species'. Well, you could be forgiven for thinking that was the title and a lot of believers in evolution either don't know or conveniently leave out the original full title. The full title is below:

ON

THE ORIGIN OF SPECIES

BY MEANS OF NATURAL SELECTION,

OR THE

PRESERVATION OF FAVOURED RACES IN THE STRUGGLE FOR LIFE.

Image is taken from CSE.

Preservation of **favoured races** in the struggle for life. Darwin used evolution as his excuse to justify his racism believing the white man was more evolved, and the black people were more like animals so treating them as such was perfectly justifiable. Very similar thinking to Nazi Germany. This was a popular thing to believe and say back then. You'd lose your job if you had this as a book title today. The modern edition conveniently omits this part.

The Bible says in Acts 17:26:

26 "**And hath made of one blood all nations of men** for to dwell on all the face of the earth, and hath determined the times before appointed, and the bounds of their habitation;"

One blood. We all come from the same source. Adam and Eve. The Bible states Eve is the mother of all living in Genesis 3:20. There is no excuse to treat someone differently. We have all been created in God's image, even those who are deeply lost. As a former atheist myself I too was once deeply lost and would mock believers quite often. I used to be one of the scoffers Peter mentions. God has worked hard on me!

It is our duty as Christians to bring the lost the gospel message, that they are in fact of worth and are not related to animals. The only relation we have to animals is that we have the same designer. Those who truly believe in Christ cannot harbour hatred in their heart and it does make me wonder about the Christians back then. Even with those who crucified our Lord, not once did he utter profanity to those who treated him the way they did. "Forgive them, for they know not what they do".

Romans 2:15:

15 "Which shew **the work of the law written in their hearts**, their conscience also bearing witness, and their thoughts the mean while accusing or else excusing one another."

We all know there is a moral law. Some are very good at suppressing it, but we all know it's there. The word conscience ironically means, with knowledge.

There are no different races. I do not like the term, there are just different skin colours, some of which contain more melanin than others. We do not describe black and white sheep as different races. They are just different colours.

A question that does come up, is where all the different skin colours come from. There are several theories on this one. One is that God mixed it all up along with the languages at the Tower of Babel. Another is that black skin is the mark of Cain, taught by the Mormon church, and the last is that it was in the gene code already, and post the flood of Noah, some areas of the earth received different levels of sunlight, so the body produces more melanin to deal with the more intense sun rays.

I lean towards it all being when God mixed up the languages at the tower of Babel. Those people teaching evolution as factual need to be careful. It does not take Einstein-level intellect to realise this religion and doctrine of evolution will damage the faith of our children. Jesus has something to say about those who cause children to sin. In Mark 9:42:

[42] "And whosoever shall offend one of these little ones that believe in me, it is better for him that a millstone were hanged about his neck, and he were cast into the sea."

Anyone leading children astray, whether that be through the teaching of evolution, or any other means, will be in trouble when they stand before God.

The Age of the Earth

The age of the earth is a more important topic than it first appears. Many Christians don't think this is something worth arguing about, but I would lovingly disagree, and, tragically, Christians are not prepared to discuss this topic and give an answer. It doesn't help that in schools only one option is taught. They do not even lay out a case for a Young Earth. This is not teaching kids how to think critically but instead teaching them what to think and not how to think.

The biggest hindrance to you obtaining the truth is the assumption that you already have it. A trap I once fell into. This is one area where many Christians are holding two conflicting ideas. This cognitive dissonance will play a big part in the falling away of the church. If you only read the Bible, you will not find millions of years in there. Jesus himself said that at the beginning, made them male and female in Matthew 19:4. In the genealogies the only dates on how long people lived are those in direct line to Jesus Christ. You can add these dates up.

The question is do you believe the words of Jesus or not? I think He would know when he made it. Many Christians ignore the glaring fact that if the earth was billions of years old, then you would get death before sin. The Bible clearly teaches that death came into the world because of man's sin and death by sin as mentioned in Romans 5:12:

12 "Wherefore, as by one man sin entered into the world, **and death by sin**; and so death passed upon all men, for that all have sinned:"

Nothing died until Adam sinned. If it had the Bible would be wrong. We die because we sin. The question is, do you believe that? Satan is an expert at lying and raising doubts in one's mind. If you want people to believe a lie you must mix it in with truth. Rat and mice poisoning is done in this way. Rat poison is 99.995% good food with only 0.005% of it being poison. Give a rat, or any creature, 100% poison they won't touch it.

One area where creationists and evolutionists do agree, however, is that the universe had a beginning and will have an end. True. The question is how did it start and how will it end? The word 'genesis' is to mean the origin or formation of something. Nearly every book in the Bible refers to Genesis. It is referenced many times in the New Testament.

Have you noticed that the order of the creation in the Bible is the total opposite of what the world teaches? When this was first pointed out to me I couldn't unsee it and I wanted to know what I was missing.

The very first verse in the Bible, clearly teaches He made the earth first. Evolution teaches the sun came first. The Bible teaches He made the oceans and then made the dry land appear. Evolution teaches the land came first. In verse 3 God produced the light, there is light **before** the sun (The last 26 verses of the Bible there is light, but no sun as He is the light giver). Evolution teaches the sun came first. The Bible teaches that it was man who brought death into the world. Evolution teaches death is what brought man into the world and that God created man, evolution says man created God. Evolution teaches there was a big bang at the start of creation, the Bible teaches there is a big bang at the end when the heavens and earth shall pass away with a great noise, a big bang.

On top of that if the earth was billions of years old then the world's population would be considerably larger. It isn't larger because the population was reduced to 8 people at the flood and has been on the rise ever since. It is widely accepted that approximately 1 billion people were on earth in 1800. However, stop believing the world is overcrowded. All 8 billion people alive today would fit into

Jacksonville in Florida, twice over. Jacksonville is the largest city by land area, covering 874 square miles, with 758 square miles of that being land.

As for England, just fly from London to Scotland and look out the window, there is plenty of land around. All of England's land which has been built on, is just 13% of the land mass, as the UK aims to protect its national parks. Incidentally, all the earth's current 8 billion population could all be drowned in Loch Ness in Scotland at the same time. The difference is there are a lot of people crammed into smaller areas such as London giving the perception it is overcrowded. The world's explosive growth population looks to have started around 4400 years ago. Which would fit the Biblical account for the end of the flood. With that rate of growth, if man had been around 3 million years we would be considerably overcrowded. Every person has two parents. They have four grandparents, eight great-grandparents. The numbers add up in a hurry! That said, God made the world to be inhabited.

Isahiah 45:18:

18 "For thus saith the LORD that created the heavens; God himself that formed the earth and made it; he hath established it, he created it not in vain, **he formed it to be inhabited**: I am the LORD; and there is none else."

He built the world to be inhabited. It is the reason He did it! Why have such a beautiful creation with nothing in it? Stop believing this world is overpopulated-nonsense, that is the world talking. God makes things multiply, that's just part of the design. Every apple has roughly five seeds. Every one of those seeds can produce an apple tree. Each tree produces hundreds of apples all having roughly five seeds per apple. You get a lot of apple trees from just one apple seed.

One objection you will hear is, where did Cain get his wife from? This question demonstrates two things. The first is the person asking has not even read the Bible, the second is they have made little or no attempt to understand it. Genesis 5:4, states Adam lived another 800 years after he had Seth and begat sons AND DAUGHTERS. Adam also lived for 900 years. How many children could you have in 900 years?! It only mentions three of them by name, Abel, Cain, and Seth. Cain would have married a sister. Many will be shocked by that but consider the fact that there was no other option, the race was genetically perfect at that point and lastly, there were no laws about intermarrying until Moses gave the law. It is only in our degraded state that intermarrying is a bad idea.

Now I can hear the objections. There are people in the world who simply do not get enough to eat. Here's the thing, there is plenty of food available. The difference is those of us who do have plenty, do not give what we have. This is also not helped by corrupt governments of the world. Roughly 1.4 billion tonnes of food go to waste EVERY year. We may not get the choice of chicken breast or thighs, but we could feed the world if we chose to. The same is true with money and land mass. There is plenty available. If a desert like Las Vegas can be populated, then why not elsewhere?

When you were a child, you will see and read books with a statement like this one:

Fossil Secrets

Fossils tell us secrets about life on Earth, millions of years ago. They can tell us how animals have changed. The elephant used to look more like a pig. How do we know? From fossils, of course!

My son brought this book home when he was five much to my annoyance. People believe it, but that doesn't make it correct. The majority have a bad track record of being wrong. There is no proof in the form of fossils. The only thing we can tell from fossils are:

The animal died.

Many animals were considerably larger in the past. We know from air samples that the earth once contained 50% more oxygen than it does today so larger animals should make sense. Creatures are limited by the amount of oxygen they can get. But no Christian should be surprised by that. Prior to the flood, there would have been considerably more vegetation on the surface.

We can test the amount of Carbon 14 in the fossil and the rate of the decay. However, it is assumed that the rate of decay has always been the same and the amount of C^{14} in the atmosphere at the time was also the same. Neither can be known.

The justification for millions of years today is something known as carbon dating. But the millions of years idea came about long before carbon dating. Carbon dating wasn't even thought about when the millions of years theory was first proposed. There are many other ways to date something but Carbon 14 is the most known and most common. When something dies it does not part mark and date stamp itself.

A fire can only burn if it has heat, fuel, and oxygen. If you change any of those variables the way and duration it will burn for will differ. We cannot know the variables of the past and would have to make several key assumptions. We know from other discoveries that the earth once had 50% more oxygen in its atmosphere. How would a forest fire react if 50% more oxygen was added to the mix?

Carbon dating was not invented until the 1940s by Willard Libby. So, when they started teaching the Earth was millions of years old back in the 1800's it was not because they had carbon-dated everything! Carbon 14 can be accurately measured by how much Carbon 14 is in the test sample. The rate of decay can also be measured. Carbon 14 is unstable, hence the radioactive nature, and is slowly breaking down. The half-life of Carbon 14 is currently 5730 (+/- 30) years. However, it is assumed that the rate of decay/breakdown has always been the same. There is no way we can know that. How would it respond if the atmosphere makeup was different? There is also the inconvenient issue that the earth's magnetic field has been measured and has been weakening roughly 5% per decade which is ten times faster than previously thought. This alone can affect the rate at which Carbon 14 is produced in the atmosphere.

Today, Earth's atmosphere contains 78% nitrogen, 21% oxygen, 0.04% carbon dioxide, and

0.00000001% radioactive carbon, otherwise known as Carbon 14 (C_{14}), yes really. This combines with the oxygen and mixes with the normal CO_2, carried by wind currents. When the sunlight encounters the Earth's atmosphere it mixes the nitrogen. Carbon has an atomic weight of 12 and nitrogen has a weight of 14 and they sit next to each other on the periodic table. Each year roughly 9.52kg is spread all over the globe as Carbon 14. Carbon 12 attaches to oxygen. The carbon attaches to the oxygen which produces carbon dioxide.

With Carbon 14 also in the atmosphere, it too mixes with the oxygen. The plants absorb this too. The animals eat the plants, and we eat the plants and animals! When an animal dies it stops eating and thus is no longer taking in the C_{14} in its food source with nothing to replace it. So, you can check the amount of C_{14} in the fossil against the amount of C_{14} **currently** in the atmosphere. The thinking is that if a fossil only has 50% of the C_{14} in it compared to the atmosphere then it's been dead for one half-life, or 5730 years. This is because the C_{14} is decaying but is no longer being replaced and will go out of balance with what is in the atmosphere. Remember the atmosphere contains 0.0000765% of C_{14}. If an animal has 0.00003825% then that would equate to 5730 years. The key point here is that it is assumed that the rate of C_{14} produced in the atmosphere has always been the same. This is something we simply cannot know.

They will teach you in schools and textbooks that coal was formed 300 million years ago. Then why is there still Carbon 14 found in the coal? In diamonds, one of the toughest substances we know, Carbon 14 has been found. Why?! It should all have reverted to Carbon 12 by now. Maybe point out that it isn't 300 million years old but the plant life that was buried under Noah's flood water 4400 years ago. A lot of people simply do not like that idea. It goes against everything they have been taught. It would also question their belief system, and people like that even less.

Carbon 14 is also forming faster than the rate of decay, meaning that it has not yet reached equilibrium. Equilibrium is the point where the amount being produced is the same as the amount of decay, so there isn't more or less and just stays balanced. If the Earth were millions of years old, we should have reached equilibrium a long time ago. It also means you cannot calculate the age of anything accurately because it was being produced at a different rate and less of it is available so of course it will test with less. It would be like having less iron in the body. Eventually, it becomes apparent that someone has less iron just by how they look!

The second law of thermodynamics tells us that everything heads towards disorder. Nothing gets better all on its own. The example of the car in the introduction is notable here. Just leave anything for an extended duration and it will rust, rot or break, and the brakes will seize. Just, by leaving it there. The Bible also backs this:

Hebrews 1:10-11:

"And, Thou Lord, in the beginning hast laid the foundation of the earth; and the heavens are the works of thine hands:

They shall perish; but thou remainest; and they all shall wax old as doth a garment."

Regardless how well you look after something, eventually it wears out. When the body starts to wear out, systems fail. The earth is doing the same. If all you did was sit in a chair and do nothing, you would wear out quickly. Everything in nature slowly gets worse. But if you read your schoolbooks, according to evolution everything is improving over time. Each generation is improving. It contradicts the laws we've known about for some time. Dare I say the complete opposite is true? We are a copy of a copy of a copy, etcetera. If you ever print a sheet of paper and then copy that copy, you'll notice that with each copy the words start to fade. Humans are the same. Each generation is getting a little worse with the passing of time, not better.

It takes real effort to make things improve. As an engineer, each newer model has had some tweaks to improve over the previous generation, and that requires effort and ingenuity. The God I worship, however, made the universe and everything in it, and He did it right the first time. As Jesus points out in Mark 12:27 and Luke 20:38, He is a God of the living. It is why He would not use evolution to improve the creation. If He did, He would not be worthy of worship as animals would have to die to improve with each generation. It would also mean that death would come before sin. That is not the God of the Bible. The God of the Bible made it right, the first time. It is our sin, disobedience, and rebellion that has brought about the current state of things.

Adding energy to anything is destructive without a mechanism that can harness the energy. The combustion chamber in a car, for example, uses the explosive force contained within the chamber to drive down the piston and create usable power for the wheels. Much of that energy is lost in both the transfer between parts and in the form of heat. It was Isaac Newton's Third Law that states that for every action, there is an equal and opposite reaction. This is still true. All these people calling for green energies are forgetting, or ignoring, that there is an opposite reaction that will occur as a result. But God will make a new heaven and new earth, so I'm not worried about it either way! Trust in that.

The only thing that can harness the energy of the sun is chlorophyll. One leaf cell is more complicated than an entire city. I am supposed to believe that happened by chance over millions of years. Yeah right! Do the people who believe this listen to themselves sometimes and release how much faith is required to believe that? I say this as someone who used to believe it because I had essentially been told what to believe, without doing the research for myself or being taught any other differing viewpoint. It was only after I started working in engineering, that I started to question what I had been taught and even to seek out answers. Life, in all its complexity, has been so finely tuned I can't not see a creator. I asked for the eyes to see and ears to hear, and I got it.

In Genesis 3:1: we read;

"Now the serpent was more subtle than any beast of the field which the Lord God had made. And he said unto the woman. Yea, **hath God said**, Ye shall not eat of every tree of the garden?' – he was trying, and successfully, raising doubts on Gods word."

Then in Genesis 3:4:

"And the serpent said unto the woman, Ye shall not surely die – Essentially calling God a liar."

It's important to look at the order and how all of this goes down. On day one, He made the light and separated the light from the darkness. On day two, He made the firmament and divided the waters which were under the firmament. On day three, He made the dry land appear and grass and herb yielding seed and tree yielding fruit. On day four, He put lights in the firmament of the heaven to divide the day and night for signs, and for seasons and the greater light to rule the day. He made the sun on day four, those believing in millions of years have a problem here as the trees were made beforehand. One day without sunlight isn't an issue. Millions of years are though. On day five, He let the waters bring forth abundantly and made the birds and filled the seas. On day six, He made man / Adam.

Then in Genesis 2, it mentions God had planted a garden and He put the man whom He had formed in the garden, then made more of each animal out of the ground for Adam to name them. By doing this Adam has seen God create things! Imagine seeing that! Keep in mind that God makes things in a different order than in chapter one. This is not a contradiction of what happened in chapter one, as some scoffers might point out, but merely what happened in the Garden of Eden only.

Then lastly God made Eve from Adam's rib and closed up the flesh. And guess what, there is only one bone in the entire human body that will grow back if it is removed. That is the lowest rib. It's like God has left us clues! And there are clues all over the scriptures for those willing to take the time to look. He made Eve last; she never saw any of that. With that in mind who did Satan go to, to deceive?! It could only have been Eve as she didn't witness any of that, and Satan uses the same tactics on us today. In 1 Timothy 2:13-14:

"For Adam was first formed then Eve.

And **Adam was not deceived** but the woman being deceived was in the transgression."

Why is this important? Firstly, the credibility of Genesis is called into question. Anyone who has never heard the evolution theory and picks up a Bible will not find millions of years in there. Also, the credibility of Jesus is at stake as He quotes from Genesis multiple times.

When you were at school, I'm willing to bet that you were taught only one option. The millions of years theory. How can one think critically if they are only taught one option? There is a surprising amount of evidence that points to a Young Earth Creation, but if you are never taught both theories you simply do not question it. You are not taught the evidence for a Young Earth Creation because that goes against the narrative and would make you question your existence and your origin. Satan, the current ruler of this age does not want that. You just go with the accepted teaching because that's all you know. Kids believe pretty much everything you tell them. Most young Western children believe a man in a red suit and white beard comes to give presents once a year, at an event called Christmas, yet many of those have no idea who Christ is!

Once a belief has been solidified it is very difficult sometimes to come back from that, nobody likes being wrong. If schools taught the evidence available for a Young Earth, then the next natural question is how did the Earth get here? What about my origin? What about dinosaurs and other fossils? But take away the millions of years and the evolution theory starts to look like what it really is. Foolish. In 2 Thessalonians 2: 10-12:

"And with all deceivableness of unrighteousness in them that perish; because they received not the love of the truth, that they might be saved.

And for this cause God shall send them strong delusion, that they should believe a lie:

That they all might be damned who believed not the truth, but had pleasure in unrighteousness.

But we are bound to give thanks alway to God for you, brethren beloved of the Lord, because God hath from the beginning chosen you to salvation through sanctification of the Spirit and belief of the truth"

It is my belief that this theory of evolution is the strong delusion mentioned in the scriptures. It means people will do as they please because they believe there are no eternal consequences to those actions. For those who believe in evolution or any other belief system, I want to ask them something. If what you believe is false, would you want to know? If they say yes, you can work with that.

As someone who was once an evolutionist, I have to eat some humble pie on this one. I held this worldview for a lot of my young life. Evolution is not something God used or would use. Firstly, it would mean that for a more advanced species to thrive everything before that would have to die when the Bible teaches that man brought death into the world, not the other way around. It is the world that teaches that. The God I worship made it all in six literal days and made it right the first time.

Romans 5:12:

[12] "Wherefore, as by one man sin entered the world, and death by sin; and so death passed upon all men, for that all have sinned."

Or Romans 6:23:

[23] **"For the wages of sin is death**; but the gift of God is eternal life through Chris Jesus our Lord."

Nothing died until Adam sinned. Adam, according to scripture lived to be 930 years old. If millions of years were true, death would come first. To teach anything else would be a clear heresy and doesn't match the other scriptures.

In 2 Peter 3:8:

⁸ "But, beloved, be not ignorant of this one thing, that one day is with the Lord as a thousand years, and a thousand years as one day."

Some people like to point to this scripture but notice two things.

It says thousand, not million.

It is simply showing that time is irrelevant to God, which is how He can declare the end from the beginning, things that are not yet done.

Or in Psalm 90:4:

⁴ "For a thousand years in thy sight are but as yesterday when it is past, and as a watch in the night."

Important things to note:

Jesus himself said in Matthew 19:4: "Have ye not read, that he which made them at the beginning made them male and female." Jesus himself said they were made male and female from the BEGINNING. So, He was either ignorant, lying or He was telling the truth... Do you believe Him?

The only times the dates were mentioned in the Bible - Adam lived to be 930 years - are those in direct genealogy to Jesus Christ. This makes it easy to add up the dates, and when you do, you'll notice that Noah's son Shem lived long enough to know Abraham for 56 years, and tell that flood story directly to Abraham, Issac, and Jacob!

The long lives of people and dates in the Bible start to drop notably after the flood. Something clearly changed in the climate. There is an old theory taught by the ancient Jews about the Earth having a crystalline firmament around it. Which would be a sheet of ice around the world. This would do several things. Firstly, it would increase the air pressure. Secondly, it would protect us from damaging UV light from the sun. Water is good at that. It has been known for some time that the Earth once had 50% more oxygen in its atmosphere.

As Christians, this should not be a surprise, before the flood came there would have been considerably more vegetation on the surface, meaning more food and land. It is not until after the flood that God instructs Noah that it's now okay to eat meat. Why? Because the vegetation that was once there is no longer there in the same quantities. Incidentally, everything you eat is linked to a plant. We eat the cow; the cow eats the grass and so forth.

Really cold ice becomes magnetic and is related to the presence of certain impurities. If a large asteroid impacted the Earth and there was an ice shield protecting it, the ice would naturally be drawn to the magnetic poles.

Question, could what we have been taught be completely wrong? Evolution teaches that we are evolving and getting better and stronger over time. Could the truth be the exact opposite? We started strong and are slowly getting worse with time? You are a copy of a copy of a copy of copy etcetera.

In Isaiah 51:6, it specifically says that the Earth shall wax old like a garment, and they that dwell therein shall die in like manner. Why are there so few human remains found when compared to other animals? Well, the first reason is found in Genesis 6:7 when God said I will destroy man. That was the point. We have become increasingly wicked with only evil in the heart continuously, kind of what is happening in society now.

The second reason is that there weren't as many people around. The third is that people tend to be smarter than other animals. We would find ways to avoid drowning. They would not fossilise if they were floating around on the top. Only creatures buried will fossilise. The Bible also mentions giants on the Earth. If people were bigger, it is possible any bones found wouldn't be recognised as human at least as we are today.

As a former atheist, I believed that when something died it went to the ground and over time would be buried by sediments, compressed, and became a fossil.

But think about that logically. Have you seen what happens to a carcass? Every scavenger tears apart the flesh and even the bones, rats, vultures, and bacteria get at it quickly and consume it long before it even has a chance to fossilise. There simply isn't time to allow for that process to even begin. Some fossils have even been found with animals partly eating other animals and even giving birth such as the one below!

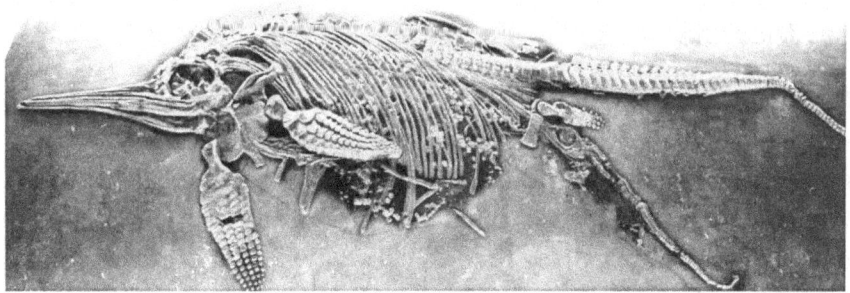

News flash, it does NOT take millions of years to give birth. These fossils are likely to have formed because they were buried quickly during a global flood. The Bible describes a worldwide flood, where the fountains of the deep broke open. You can open YouTube or Rumble and watch how water behaves during a flood. The speed of the water mixes up so many sediments that it shapes the land and can bury everything in its path. Despite what we are taught in schools there is no evidence of missing links. Not only that but the number of fossils we find suggests they were buried quickly. They cannot fossilise if they are left in the open air.

Fossils of clams have also been found on the top of Mount Everest. Thousands of these clams are closed. When clams die, they open. These clams would have to have been buried quickly. How did they even get to the top of a mountain anyway? In Proverbs 8:25 it mentions before the mountains were settled.

I am an engineer, with a passionate love of motorbikes. If you put 100 bikes in a room with no logos, I could work out who made most of them. They are made by the same group of engineers and leave similar design characteristics as a result. We did not evolve from a single-celled organism. But we do all have the same designer, and it shows.

The Dinosaurs

Now one question that will 100% come up when discussing how old the earth is, is the dinosaurs, and we as Christians better have some good answers. The word 'dinosaur' wasn't invented until 1841 by Sir Richard Owen. In 1891, 50 years later the word 'dinosaur' still does not appear in the English dictionary. I've touched on the definitions of words changing in other areas of this book. But the word 'dinosaur' did not exist in 1611 when the KJV was translated. The word 'dragon' did though. The word 'dragon' is in the Bible 35 times.

Why are there so many legends of people slaying dragons throughout history? St. George is famous for slaying a dragon, the Welsh flag is a dragon. The Chinese calendar features 11 real animals and one mythical one. Could there have been 12 when that calendar was first drawn up? Why is that so hard for some people to believe? We know that the Earth once had 50% more oxygen within its atmosphere. Reptiles never stop growing. They grow throughout their lifetime. The Bible says that Adam lived to be 930. What would happen to a crocodile if you gave it 50% more oxygen and allowed it to live for over 900 years? Something like an archosaur?

One of the largest swamps on Earth is in the Republic of Congo called the Likouala swamp. It is largely unexplored and covers 55,000 square miles. The locals describe something like a crocodile which is 50 feet long. They call it Mahamba. They also speak of another creature they call Mokele-Mbembe, they sketch something like the below:

Now why would they sketch that? They describe them as about 20 feet from nose to tail, nocturnal, and spend most of their time in the water. But isn't it smaller than we expect? With less oxygen in today's atmosphere, this size should not be a surprise.

Why is it that the brontosaurus had nostrils the same size as modern-day horses? Considering this animal was 24 meters tall (80 feet) if it were to be put in our atmosphere today, it would suffocate in no time. We also know that insects and other creatures we see today were once much larger in the past. The amount of oxygen in the atmosphere limits how big something can grow. The plants produce the oxygen. Pre-flood there would have been more oxygen as there would have been more plant life than there is now. Post-flood we have had less plant life and as a result less oxygen so life cannot grow as big as it once was.

Several stones were discovered in Peru in 1571 by the Spanish, known as the Ica stones, which you can search for yourself through a web search. Several of these have images of what we today would call dinosaurs. How could they have been drawn on there if the people had not seen one, and why are people drawn on there with them? Bones do not tell you what the skin is like, but these images show patterns on the creatures. There are also many mosaics around the world which display dragons. The Vikings used dragon heads on their ships. Why? And why, would modern depictions of these animals, show them having feathers? The world wants you to think they were 'evolving' into the modern-day bird, which is frankly absurd.

DO YOU REALLY TRUST THE LORD?

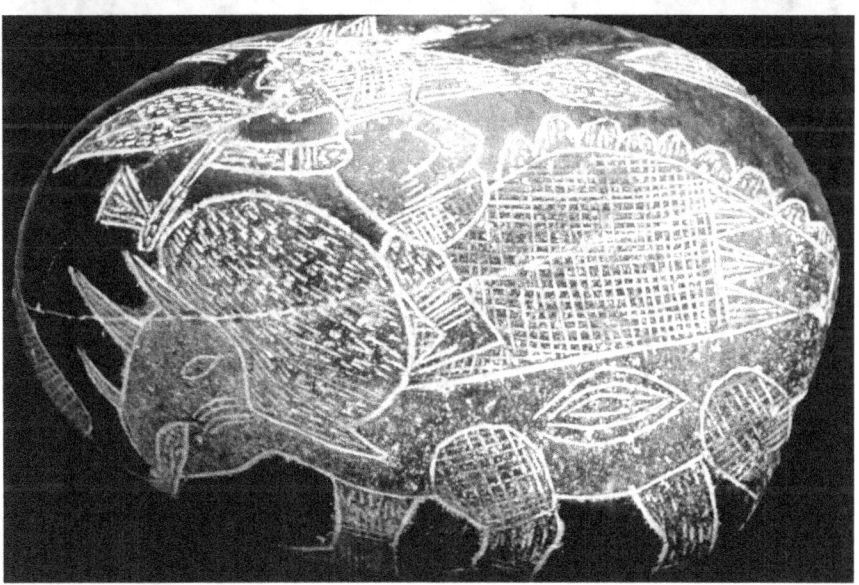

(Previous Page) This stone has a person riding a dinosaur. Maybe that's how they moved big stones and built Stonehenge? It also looks like it has something on its back like we would put a saddle on a horse.

(Above) Why are there circles on the side of this one? Bones do not tell you what the skin was like. Fossilised dinosaur skin has been found which also had circle patterns on the side. Whoever carved this must have seen a live one.

Image of someone riding a 'dinosaur', or dragon, in their eyes.

I think we've been lied to and deceived in our schools. They teach that no one has ever seen a dinosaur, yet here are images of people riding them. There is no way we can know that without speaking to everyone who has ever lived. The Bible says that God made ALL of creation in six days. The question is, do you believe that? Dinosaurs and man have been around together since the beginning. There are also many legends of sea monsters. Lock Ness comes to mind! There have been over 11000 sightings of the Loch Ness monster in Scotland. When the road alongside the Loch was first built in 1933 there were 52 separate sightings of the Loch Ness Monster. Why would all these people risk personal ridicule unless they did see something?

There are also many legends in the tropical and subtropical regions of Africa called the Kongamato, to a Westerner, this is a pterosaur/pterodactyl-looking creature. Now I've not covered every square inch of the earth. I've also never seen a Dodo. Just because you haven't seen something it does not mean that they don't still exist somewhere. So, what happened to the dinosaurs and sea monsters of legend?

In England, we don't have many dangerous creatures anymore. They have either been killed to not be a threat to our children or the rising English Channel prevented them from crossing over. As for the dinosaurs, I would suggest that after the flood, their numbers would have been considerably lessened. Men likely hunted them for food and the less dangerous ones to move heavy things around. The lowering oxygen would limit their size and as they got smaller; our uses for them had changed. Our ancestors may not even recognise it as a dinosaur/dragon anymore. What would a crocodile look like if we let it live to be 900 years old and increase the oxygen in the atmosphere?

One of the things the early settlers had to do before building the town, is drive away the ferocious animals or most likely, kill them. St. George is famous for slaying a dragon, and we still celebrate him today at St. Georges Day. You don't want them taking away your young, so they need to be removed. In the USA there used to be hundreds of bears and buffalos. Not so anymore.

As for the legendary sea monsters, back in the days when these sightings were common, we sailed around on our ships with a big mast being pulled by nothing other than the wind. The Kraken, one of the most well-known sea monsters, is described as something akin to an octopus of monstrous size. Giant squids have now been found in the ocean depths. The ocean is one of the least explored places on

Earth. Many logbooks from old crossings report many of such sea monsters. Back then, ships travelled by sail and wind. They made no noise. Today we sail around using big diesel-powered engines. These creatures would hear and feel us coming for miles. Is it any wonder we don't see these legendary monsters on the surface now? Especially those more sensitive to it. And, with so little of the ocean explored, I wouldn't be surprised if a legendary monster is still lurking down there.

In Isaiah 27:1:

[1] "In that day the LORD with his sore and great and strong sword shall punish leviathan the piercing serpent, even leviathan that crooked serpent; and **he shall slay the dragon that is in the sea.**"

Larger People and Life-forms

More oxygen makes the life forms bigger, including people. The monster stones of Baalbek are huge, the block in the image below is 71 feet long, 14 feet high, 13 feet wide, and is estimated to weigh 15000 tonnes. Who or what is shaping and moving a block this size? There are two camels and multiple people on and around it for scale!

The Bible says in Genesis 6:4:

⁴ "There were giants in the earth in those days;"

Could everything we've been taught in our schools be a lie? Everything gets worse over time, oxygen has decreased, could we have started big and are slowly getting worse and more restricted with the decreasing of oxygen? Could they have even used bigger animals? We know animals were once much larger. Could they have even used dragons, or what we would consider to be dinosaurs to move them? We have no idea how our ancestors were able to move such stones. The biggest crane today can lift roughly 5000 tonnes. These stones make that weight look pathetic. I now believe they used much larger lifeforms to move them while being bigger themselves. They would certainly be strong enough!

Not so Stupid

Our predecessors were not as stupid as our textbooks would like us to believe. The rock above is one such example. The textbooks want us to think that we started off dumb and are slowly getting smarter with the many inventions we have today. The reality is that evidence would suggest we were smarter in the past, the last 100 years or so being an exception. I remember reading books showing images of tools where one was better than the other as 'we learned' how to make better tools.

When I first started working in engineering, I started in sheet metal, it didn't take long to see that the standard of work was better with some colleagues than others. Some were naturally good at making things, some hurried, and even today the quality of the work is plain to see between individuals. When I look at these images of weapons and tools from the past, it becomes obvious to me that many factors need to be factored in, such as time available, materials used, and even the natural skill of the person making the tool or weapon.

In the book of Daniel, it was predicted knowledge would increase in the end times and the invention of the internet has certainly done that. But why is the knowledge that made the pyramids gone? Just the pyramids are a wonder. Those stones are so tight you cannot pass a piece of paper through them. There are no obvious entry points. These stones would have to have been cut, but I am not aware of any machine that would cut stones like that so accurately, even with the entrance not being discovered until 1800 AD!

We find similarly cut stones in the ancient city of Sacsahuaman which was once part of the Inca civilisation. They clearly had knowledge that we no longer possess today. Again, using my background, I can see how this might be the case. One is because as time passes, we are regressing and getting worse, not better. Second, is that many people like to retain certain knowledge to themselves and not share it. This is to feel like they are important and makes them feel valuable. As a result, the knowledge is lost over time. I have seen this happen in real time in more than one engineering company.

The famous Nazca lines in Peru feature images of animals and insects which are not only incredibly accurate but very straight. It is not possible to view these images from the ground. They can only be seen from the air. Suggesting that our ancestors were far from stupid. They would have known that hot air is less dense than cold air, thus something like a hot air balloon is well within the realm of possibility to view the images from the air. One of the most interesting images in the lines is the 'spider'. What is even more interesting in the image is this spider has one leg longer than the other. This spider can be found in caves, has poor vision, and this one leg extends so it can exchange its DNA with the female, and it is the correct leg too.

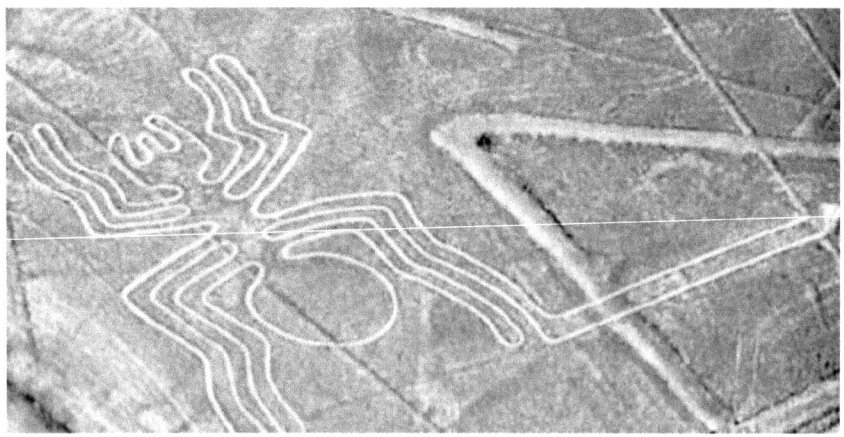

But what if they did indeed know how to get airborne? The image below is currently in a museum in the USA and is referred to as a stylised insect! I've been working in aerospace engineering for most of my working life, if people really believe this to be a stylised insect, I do not know what to say to them and would suggest they are deceiving themselves. This is quite clearly an aircraft concept and suggests they at least knew about flight.

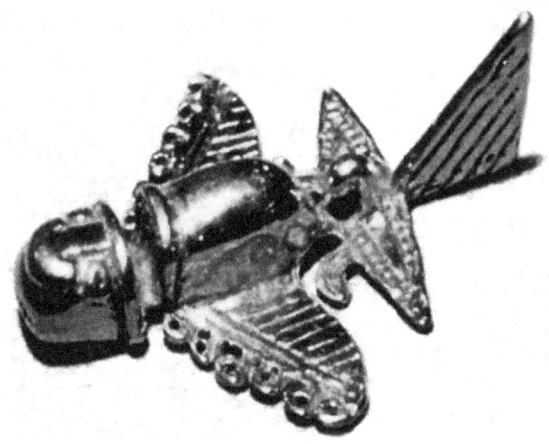

Or this one:

Today we use mechanical engines to power our aircraft. They clearly knew about the concept, and they certainly could have used a different power source.

Other well-known items that have been found such as the Baghdad Battery. The oldest battery known to man and found in 1936. The Egyptians too knew something about electricity on some of their hieroglyphics showing eels in tubes with a wire and some kind of generator. It has been theorised that the pyramids were used to generate electricity.

The hieroglyphics also show many modern-day technologies:

We can see what looks like a helicopter, boat or submarine, and even what could be described as a UFO. Maybe a blimp or something that hasn't been invented yet!

The Antikythera mechanism (Image Right) is a very well-known device that was found at the bottom of the Aegean Sea with an analogue computing device as shown below. Our ancestors were not stupid. What we need today is not what they needed during their time.

There is every reason to suspect that these different cultures sprung out of the scattering of the peoples of Babel. After the flood, God gave instructions to scatter across the earth. In Genesis 11:4:

⁴ "And they said, Go to, let us build us a city and a tower, whose top may reach unto heaven; and let us make us a name, **lest we be scattered** abroad upon the face of the whole earth."

The people wanted to build the tower to prevent being scattered. This was against God's will, so He made them scatter. When the people scattered could they have taken much of the knowledge of Babel with them, sadly over time, much of this knowledge has been lost to time.

Other interesting points to consider are areas such as the Grand Canyon in the USA. We are told the Grand Canyon formed over millennia, yet there are no visible erosion marks in the rock faces. Just for a bit of fun, compare images of the Grand Canyon and a modern-day copper mine. You won't be able to unsee the striking similarity. I highly suspect that the Grand Canyon was once used for mining certain minerals that once rested there, with certain parts of the Grand Canyon being off-limits to the public.

Adam and Eve would not have needed what we today need. They had everything to eat, and drink and the animals did not harm them. That means they wouldn't need a house to live in, nor a car to travel to work and visit family. Everything they need is outside, safe to reside in with a perfect climate.

The Limiting Factor

The concept of a limiting factor is crucial in various scientific disciplines, including ecology, chemistry, and physiology. It refers to the component or condition that restricts the growth, abundance, or distribution of an organism or a population in an ecosystem, the rate of a chemical reaction, etcetera. An example of course is above. Insects, reptiles, and other organisms are limited in how big they can grow based on the amount of oxygen they can receive. You can test this by putting a tiny goldfish in a bowl in your house, then move it to a pond outside. You'll notice in the pond it will grow considerably larger.

During intense exercise, the amount of oxygen your muscles can get will affect your performance. Understanding the limiting factor is crucial for optimising growth, performance, and yield and allows engineers and managers to make informed decisions to mitigate constraints. There are many ways to tell how old the earth is, some numbers are large, and some are small. Pay attention to the small numbers. For our plants and animals, Liebig's Law of the Minimum applies, which states that the growth of a plant is limited by the scarcest nutrient (the limiting factor), rather than the total amount of resources available. Our plants and animals today are limited by the amount of oxygen they can receive. That wasn't the case before the flood when the water was contained under the surface meaning more plant life on the surface, thus creating more oxygen.

Sun Math

The sun is a constantly running engine. It has mass made from its fuel. It burns hydrogen and converts it into light and heat energy. Light and heat DO NOT carry any mass. Hydrogen does, however. That is a big problem for the millions of years theory for several reasons. According to NASA the sun consumes 600 million tonnes of hydrogen per **second. With a mass loss of around 4 million tonnes EVERY second.**

Since 1836 over 100 different observations of the sun have been conducted by the Royal Greenwich Observatory and the U.S. Naval Observatory with direct and visual measurements. With the measurements reading that the sun's diameter is shrinking at a rate of five feet per hour or a rate of approx. 0.1% every century.

"The Sun consumes about 600 million tons of hydrogen per second. That's 6×10^8 tonnes. For comparison, the mass of the Earth is about 1.35×10^{21} tonnes. This would mean the Sun consumes the mass of the Earth in about 70,000 years."

Dr. Louis Barbier (NASA)

"It is incorrect to say that the Sun is shrinking, and it has been since the 'creation' of the Universe. The Sun is not shrinking at a consistent rate. The data that were used to derive that was both wrong and misinterpreted.

Dr Eric Christian

Fill your car up with fuel and leave it to run at a constant pace it will eventually use up its fuel and the engine will stop. The car will be lighter in weight too!

Points to ponder:

If you were a 300lbs person and lost 10lbs a day how long would it take for you to look visibly different? You simply cannot keep losing. Eventually, you will cease to function. To say the sun remains unchanged in size and gravitation influence is simply unreasonable. You do not need Einstein-level intellect to work out the sun would have to have been bigger in the past.

If light and heat carry no mass, but hydrogen does, how has the earth remained in the same orbit allowing life to flourish for 'millions of years? Mass is directly proportional to gravity. If the sun and earth were millions of years old, then the gravitational pull of the sun would be considerably greater and suck the earth in.

NASA states that the sun burns 600 million tonnes of hydrogen every second in an energy transfer from gas through a fusion burning process, converts and expels the matter into heat and light energy and does so at a consistent rate. But according to NASA, the sun isn't shrinking at a constant rate. Seriously? How many laws of physics does that break?

The fact is the sun's hydrogen is being used up meaning gravity should be weakening with the loss of mass and it should be shrinking too. To say otherwise goes against everything else we observe in nature.

In Genesis 1:11-19 God says the grass, the herb-yielding seed, and the fruit tree were made on day three. He made the sun on day four. If millions of years were true the plants might struggle to cope in darkness for millions of years, they will cope just fine for a day with no problem. The same is true for the insects that pollinate the plants.

It has been estimated that there are enough stars out in the universe that every person could own 11 trillion of them! They are just the stars that are known about. At that rate, if the universe were old that would mean a star would need to form at a rate of 6,655,00 every minute. Nobody has ever seen a star form. We have only witnessed them exploding.

You'll notice in some books they tell you that the stars form in a nebula in clouds of gas and dust. But that would break Boyle's Gas Law, discovered in 1662. When gasses are squeezed together, pressure and temperature build until it drives the gasses apart again. Nobody ever has seen gas collapsing into a solid. Not ever. Boyles Gas Law acts like a magnet, when it gets too close, it repels. If you spot a new point of light in the night sky, just maybe the cloud in front of it has cleared so now you can see what was already there. There have been times in England when the fog has been so thick I cannot see the signs and road markings in my street. But they become visible again when the fog clears.

Moon Math

The moon has been known to be moving away from the Earth for a while. It is moving away from the earth at the rate of 1.5 inches per year since it has been measured by NASA since 1969. Anyone who is actually thinking will know that means it had to have been closer in the past. This presents a problem as the moon causes the tides on the Earth's surface and has an impact on our planet. It also acts as a balancing counterweight, to prevent the Earth from 'wobbling' in space.

The tides are calculated by the moon's distance to the Earth, with the closest and farthest it gets, during orbit. You can then add back the years at the rate of 1.5 inches per year. With gravity, the closer it is the quicker it will be sucked in by the larger of the two bodies. Just like when you bring two magnets closer together the real numbers would be considerably larger. With the moon closer, the tides would be higher.

We'd also need to consider the sun's gravitational influence if all the sun's mass was added back into the equation. There is also an inconvenient law known as the Roche Limit where two planetary bodies become too close, the larger of the two will tear apart the smaller of the two bodies. For the earth and moon, this has been calculated to be 9500 kilometres. There is a law known as the Inverse Square Law, this law applies to light, sound, electromagnetic fields, and gravity. Newton's Law of Universal Gravitation states that the force between two masses is inversely proportional to the square of the distance between them. If the distance between two objects is doubled, the gravitational force between them is reduced to a quarter. If you bring the moon in closer to two-thirds of the distance though that effect will increase by 2.25 times.

Point to ponder:

The moon moving away from the Earth affects both the tides and the stability of the Earth in space. What effect is this having on the planet and climate? It is estimated at 10 million years the tide could be more than 376 feet high. In Japan in 2010 we could see what a 128 feet tidal wave could do.

Gravity acts like a magnet, bringing the moon in closer and the closer it gets the quicker it gets pulled in. This would increase the gravitational force on our world. Closer still and we run the risk of having the moon break apart once hitting the Roche Limit. We observed this in action, when in 1994 the comet Shoemaker-Levy 9 came too close to the planet Jupiter and broke into 21 large individual fragments, before being sucked into the planet.

The Earth's Rotation Speed

The earth rotates on its axis with a speed being approximately 1037 mph at the equator. But the earth is slowing down. Many people know about the 'leap' year where we have an extra day in February every 4 years to catch up. But we also have a leap second, that many have never even heard of. We have a leap second every 1 to 1.5 years. One of the reasons it is slowing down is because the moon is moving away from the Earth. The moon exerts a gravitational pull on the Earth's oceans, creating the tides, as the Earth rotates these tidal bulges are slightly ahead of the line connecting the Earth and Moon, which creates a torque, slowing the Earth's rotation and increasing our days.

The earth is spinning, and is slowing down, you don't need to be a genius to work out that at one point it had to be spinning quicker.

Now if the earth is young, this doesn't present a problem. Adam and Eve would've had a shorter day. But if the earth were millions of years old, now you have a big problem. The Coriolis Effect would be extreme, with winds approaching 1000 mph, like the planets in the outer solar system. We simply could not survive under such conditions.

The Earth's Magnetic Field

The Earth's magnetic field is weakening, a phenomenon that has been observed over the past several centuries. The strength of the Earth's magnetic field has been measured and monitored for more than 180 years. Data from the geomagnetic observations and satellites show that the field has been gradually weakening by 5% - 10% per century. One particular region where this weakening is more pronounced is the South Atlantic Anomaly (SAA), an area where the magnetic field is significantly weaker than in other parts of the world. This weakening has been increasing over time and is a subject of ongoing study.

The implications of a weaker magnetic field cannot be overstated. The magnetic field acts as a shield against solar and cosmic radiation. A weaker field means this protection is reduced, which can affect satellites, communications, and power grids and the accurate measurements of the atmosphere can differ (like Carbon 14). It also means increased radiation for us on the surface. It has been suggested that the magnetic field is experiencing a pattern of reversal, however, I do not buy into that narrative for the reasons of the fact the Earth is waxing old as the Bible describes. As something ages it wears out, we can observe that in every other aspect of nature, from the car we buy to our own fragile bodies.

The Flood

Today our planet is over 70% surface water. In the original creation, I wouldn't be surprised if were the other way around with 70% land as the water was under the surface of the earth. We know that there was once 50% more oxygen. More trees and vegetation would produce more oxygen. This would allow pretty much everything to grow bigger. One thing we do know from fossils found is animals did indeed grow larger. Dragonflies once had a five-meter wingspan!

A Japanese physicist by the name of Dr. Kei Mori conducted an experiment where he filtered a tomato plant with ultraviolet rays and pressurised the CO_2 under a plastic dome to simulate the pre-flood world. That tomato plant grew 16 feet tall and produced over 900 tomatoes from ONE plant. It ended up having scaffolding just to hold it up! It ended up growing 40 feet tall and produced 15,000 tomatoes from that one plant! The plant was for cherry tomatoes, but this cherry tomato plant produced tomatoes that were tennis ball-sized.

The Bible dates from the start of creation to the start of the flood, adding up to 1656. You can add these up yourself by using the genealogies in the Bible by adding up the ages of the patriarchs at the birth of their first sons and then include the time until the flood.

Patriarch	Age at Son's Birth	Lifespan	Notable Son
Adam	130	930	Seth
Seth	105	912	Enosh
Enosh	90	905	Kenan
Kenan	70	910	Mahalalel

Mahalalel	65	895	Jared
Jared	162	962	Enoch
Enoch	65	365	Methuselah
Methuselah	187	969	Lamech
Lamech	182	777	Noah
Noah	502	950	Shem
Shem	100	600	Arphaxad
Arphaxad	35	438	Shelah
Shelah	30	433	Eber
Eber	34	464	Peleg
Peleg	30	239	Reu
Reu	32	239	Serug
Serug	30	230	Nahor
Nahor	29	148	Terah
Terah	70	205	Abraham
Abraham	100	175	Isaac
Isaac	60	180	Jacob
Jacob	91	147	Joseph
Joseph	-	110	-

Genealogical Ages from Adam to Noah:

Adam to Seth: 130 years (Genesis 5:3)

Seth to Enosh: 105 years (Genesis 5:6)

Enosh to Kenan: 90 years (Genesis 5:9)

Kenan to Mahalalel: 70 years (Genesis 5:12)

Mahalalel to Jared: 65 years (Genesis 5:15)

Jared to Enoch: 162 years (Genesis 5:18)

Enoch to Methuselah: 65 years (Genesis 5:21)

Methuselah to Lamech: 187 years (Genesis 5:25)

Lamech to Noah: 182 years (Genesis 5:28-29)

Noah's AGE AT THE TIME OF THE FLOOD: 600 years (Genesis7:6)

In the chart above notice how the lifespans drop notably after the flood. That suggests a radical change in climate! God has laid out the timescale in the Bible for you by adding up the genealogies from Adam to Abraham, Abraham to Jesus, and Jesus to the Present day, totalling 6000 years since the creation. Jesus is speaking to the Pharisees and says in Mark 10:6:

6 "But from the beginning of the creation God made them male and female."

Throughout the Bible, God says He made it all in six days, even those versions that try to squirm out of it! Adam was made on day six and the dates given to when they lived are in direct line to Jesus Christ. The question is do you believe what God's Word says?

There are nearly 300 separate worldwide flood legends throughout the world. It is not contained only in biblical scripture. Hawaii and China have legends where that describe a great flood that almost wiped out humanity with only one family surviving. Both have legends of a worldwide flood.

But there are many more which I would encourage you to seek for yourself.

In Genesis 7:11:

11 "In the six hundredth year of Noah's life, in the second month, the seventeenth day of the month, the same day were all the **foundations of the great deep broken up**, and the windows of heaven were opened."

Maybe this is the real reason why the earth has fault lines, the fountains of the deep broke open. In

July 2023 the Indy100 website ran a headline that said: "Massive ocean discovered beneath the Earth's crust containing more water than on the surface." As a Christian, this does not surprise me at all. The majority of the surface water originally came from under the surface. Psalm 24:1-2: would seem to suggest that:

"The earth is the LORD's, and the fulness thereof; the world, and they that dwell therein.

For he hath founded it upon the seas, and established it upon the floods."

Psalms 136:6:

6 "To him that **stretched out the earth above the waters**: for his mercy endureth for ever."

2 Peter 3:5-6:

"For this they willingly are ignorant of, that by the word of God the heavens were of old, and **the earth standing out of the water and in the water**:

⁶Whereby the world that then was, being overflowed with water, perished."

Willingly ignorant in Greek means 'dumb on purpose'. In Proverbs 5:15 it talks about drinking water out of your own cistern and your own well. Implying water was taken from underground. Many ancient cultures such as Ancient Mesopotamia (modern-day Iraq), Egypt, and many others depended on wells to provide access to groundwater for drinking and other purposes. There are many subterranean lakes in the world, God did indeed stretch the earth above the waters!

We've all heard of the supposed supercontinent of Pangea. This theory is that all the continents were once connected as one big supercontinent before being broken up by the fault lines. But I now believe this is wrong. The continents are all still connected. There is just a body of water in the low areas. The English Channel is a body of water that separates southern England and northern France with a width of 21 miles at the narrowest point. The deepest point is 174 meters an average of 120 meters. If the level went down by 28.5 meters, you would be able to walk to France, and thus the rest of Europe and surrounding nations. At one point I would agree it was all connected, but that was because the water on the surface was once under the surface.

There is a large sinkhole in Leye County in China which contains trees growing as tall as 130 feet, in a sinkhole! It is 630 feet deep and made up of 5 million cubic meters. The trees get their water from UNDER the surface's crust. It is theorised and is my belief too, that trees, plants, and we people would get most of their water from below the crust of the earth when God first made it. There is a reason so many ancient societies used wells for drinking water with the

Bible talking about getting water from your OWN well, coming from subterranean lakes and oceans.

After the flood we read in Genesis 8:1: "...and God made a wind to pass over the earth, and the waters asswaged." – the word asswaged means to sink down. Water will naturally find the path of least resistance and as water is heavy it will flow to the softer materials and weigh it down much like the below image.

Today the water we see on the surface of our planet is the leftover water from the flood. Some of it has sunk back under the surface. Pre-flood there would have been more oxygen and greater air pressure. The water we now see on the surface was once inside the crust of the earth. With more oxygen, people and animals would grow bigger. It has been known for some time that the earth once had more oxygen in its atmosphere. With more land and less surface water would result in food being more readily available.

Now I hear a lot of scoffers when it comes to the flood of Noah. How did they bring all those species of <insert animal here> on the Ark? Noah did not need to bring every type of animal on the Ark. He was only required to bring one of every sort/kind and only those whose nostrils were the breath of life and in the dry land. That means no insects or any ocean-dwelling creature. He was also 600 years old at the time of the flood. Anyone with common sense should be able to work out that you do not bring full-sized animals! You bring babies or young infants. Little ones sleep more, eat less, bounce better, and will live longer once the flood is over to repopulate the earth. Which was the reason he was required to take them on the Ark to start with!

In Genesis 6:19:

19 "And of every living thing of all flesh, two of every sort shalt thou bring into the Ark, to keep them alive with thee; they shall be male and female."

Then again in Genesis 7:14-15:

"They, and every beast **after his kind**, and all the cattle **after their kind**, and every creeping thing that creepeth upon the earth **after his kind**, and every fowl after his kind, every bird of every sort.

And they went in unto Noah into the ark, two and two of all flesh, wherein is the **breath of life**."

Genesis 7:22:

22 "All in whose **nostrils was the breath of life, of all that was in the dry land**, died."

He just had to make sure he had a male and a female. From there we get all the other varieties of offspring. We are all descendants of Adam and Eve, yet as humans, we have black skin, white skin, curly hair, straight hair, blonde, redhead, tall people, short people, etcetera. All of that from just two people. All of that had to be in the gene code to start with. In all my years I haven't once seen a dog give birth to a cat or a chicken lay a sparrow! Nobody I have met has ever witnessed an animal produce a different kind of animal.

But if you believe in evolution that totally happened at some point, we just need faith that it did. Question, if we came from a bacterium to a fish, to an amphibian to a reptile, and a mammal, (or FARM for easy reference) then why do all these things still exist? They should have become higher beings by now. Or it just didn't happen to start with. The theory of evolution is a form of religious belief, yet those who follow it somehow cannot see it. Every person on earth is religious, but only a handful know that.

At some point though God will restore the creation. Isaiah 11:6-7:

6 "The wolf also shall dwell with the lamb, and the leopard shall lie down with the kid; and the calf and the young lion and the fatling together; and a little child shall lead them.

7 And the cow and the bear shall feed; their young ones shall lie down together: **and the lion shall eat straw like the ox."**

Lion eating straw? Sounds like the creation will return to everything being vegetarian again. In 1946 a female African lion known as "Little Tyke" was famous for refusing to eat meat of any kind and rejected it when her owners tried to introduce it into her diet! Despite not eating meat she was in excellent health with no deficiencies. She was also known for her gentle and affectionate nature, very different from 99% of lions! This is what all creatures in the original creation would have been like, and what it will one day go back to.

2 Peter 3:13:

13 "Nevertheless we, according to his promise, look for **new heavens and a new earth**, wherein dwelleth righteousness."

And again, in Revelation 21:1

21 "And I saw a new heaven and a new earth: for the first heaven and the first earth were passed away; **and there was no more sea.**"

Once the flood was over there was considerably less vegetation, before the flood everything ate plants and would again when God restored everything. It wasn't until after the flood that God told Noah to eat meat and the 'fear and dread of you' became apparent. Interestingly, everything you eat is indeed linked to a plant of some kind! It is also interesting to note that before the flood people were living to be 900 years old. There are many legends of people living to be 1000.

But read your Bible and you will notice that after the flood the ages that they were living started to go down. It goes from 900 before the flood, then 600, then 400, then 200 post-flood. You'd be lucky to make it to 100 years old today and even then, you'd probably not want to. Now that was a change in climate! It also meant the oxygen levels went down so that animals and vegetation were more limited in how big they could grow and that was reflected in the fossils found versus what we see in today's world.

What about the Ark itself? The Ark only really had one requirement. It had to float and that's it, so it didn't need sails or a rudder and likely would have made use of drogue stones. These would stabilise the Ark during rough periods. The whole world was going to be underwater, so it didn't need any more than that. Some theorise it may also have contained a moonpool for stability and acting as a piston pumping air through.

But where is the Ark now? There are several theories as to where it is now. One theory is that it was taken apart and the wood was reused to build shelter. Another is that it rotted over time, and the third is that it is in Turkey at Mount Ararat. There is a boat-like formation near the city of Dogubeyazit in Turkey and Turkey recognised it as the remains of Noah's Ark in 1987, even having a visitors' centre there. It at least measures the right size and drogue stones were found nearby with iron rivets detected within the 'wreckage'. It would also indicate it has bowed out over time, which is expected. I haven't visited this site myself, however.

Above is the image some believe to be the remains of the Ark.

Another theory is that the Ark was broken down and used for other things, such as building a house. This is what I would've done as everything outside has been destroyed and now the animals will not be as friendly! But where was God in all this chaos?!

In Genesis 7:1:

¹ And the LORD said unto Noah, **Come thou** and all thy house **into the ark**; for thee have I seen righteous before me in this generation.

Genesis 8:16:

¹⁶ **Go forth** of the ark, thou, and thy wife, and thy sons, and thy sons' wives with thee.

The words used here, God said, 'Come', and then 'Go forth'. Like welcoming Noah in and seeing him out. God was with them for the whole 15 months they were in the Ark. How would you be knowing God is with you in times of hardship?

Time

The topic of time is one of great fascination for me. The importance of the discovery by Albert Einstein that time is a physical property cannot be overstated. Gravity itself can affect time, also known as Gravitational Time Dilation. This can be demonstrated by the two atomic clocks based in the National Institute of Standards and Technology (NIST) in Boulder, Colorado. The other is at the Royal Observatory in Greenwich, England. These clocks are identical. They are accurate to 1 second per million years! This is because they are based on the $Cesium_{133}$ atom = (9,192,631,770 Hz). It is this accuracy that allows for GPS navigation to be possible. These two clocks are different every year by five microseconds, with the NIST clock being

5 µseconds FASTER than the same clock in Greenwich. Both clocks are CORRECT! This is because time itself can vary at different altitudes, gravitational influence, and speed.

The clock at Boulder is at an altitude of 5400 feet while the clock at Greenwich is at 80 feet. The clocks are different because of differences in gravity. Raising an atomic clock by 1 meter would increase it by 10^{-16} every meter of elevation, that is 10 with 16 zeros after it! It is both predictable and measurable. The speed at which you travel also has an impact on the effect of time. It is worth reading about the 1971 experiment where two aircraft went in opposite directions, and the clocks on board were different upon landing. The point is that time itself is NOT uniform and varies with gravity, mass, speed, etcetera.

Everything we see decays. A house or vehicle will degrade as time passes. Even if you bought a brand-new car and then left it on your drive, or in a garage, for 20 years without driving it once, would it even start, and still drive as well as if it were new? Would a house stay looking new without any maintenance? We observe that time makes things degrade. It does not make things improve.

I have worked in manufacturing for many years, and many skills have been lost over time. Some key workers like to hold their knowledge in the fear if they teach someone else, they are less valuable and can be replaced. To this day, nobody really knows how the Egyptian pyramids were built. That knowledge has been lost. How those blocks are so closely fitted together that a piece of paper will not even go through is extraordinary!

The older I get, the more acutely aware I am of my own mortality. It is something I think about often. When we are young, we feel almost invincible. We do not think about how long we will live for. In the Western world today life expectancy can vary but 75 – 85, which is very short especially when you compare it to Adam! Our days are numbered. In Hebrews 9:27:

27 "And as it is appointed unto men once to die, but after this the judgement."

Psalm 90:12:

12 "So teach us to number our days, that we may apply our hearts unto wisdom."

We have an appointment with God, but we do not know that date. Satan has focused a lot of his efforts on filling our time with worldly pleasures and activities. The busier we are the less we focus on God, His purposes, and our appointment!

What is hard for us to fathom is that God is not contained within our time domain. He is outside of it. He is right now in tomorrow. It is how He can see the end from the beginning. Time, as we know it, does not pass for God. He can see the past, present, and future all at the same time. Like a helicopter over a river. God can see from above, all the turns in the river, the calm parts and the turbulent parts all at the same time. If you radio up to the helicopter you can find out the best path to take, even if you cannot see it yet.

Suppose you watch a movie, and you know the full story and what will happen. When you show your friends, they don't know you already know the outcome of the story. God at this point isn't controlling the characters of the film, but He knows what they are all going to do. The characters in the movie do not know their actions at certain points until it happens, and the observer has no control or knowledge of the events. Like a video game. I can play a video game and see the 'world' within and be completely outside of the game's world and its rules. God declares in Isaiah 46:10:

¹⁰ **"Declaring the end from the beginning, and from ancient times the things that are not yet done**, saying, My counsel shall stand, and I will do all my pleasure"

NOTE: A light year is a measurement of distance. It is not actually related to time.

Ignorance

Evil always existed. It is the other side of the coin. Goodness cannot exist without evil. God chose to keep Adam and Eve ignorant of what evil was. Keeping that from them was for their benefit. I have two children, nine and four at the time of writing. We do not have the news on in our house. It is forbidden. Why? Because God kept Adam and Eve ignorant about evil, on purpose. At that time, Adam did not even know what evil was! I do not want my children to be exposed to the sins and evils of the world. I want to shield them from it for as long as possible. I accept I cannot do that forever in this sin-filled evil world but I'm going to prevent it as long as I can.

Faith is important as without it, it is impossible to please Him (Hebrews 11:6), but that doesn't mean that our faith should be blind. Do not confuse faith with ignorance. Do all you can to fix your ignorance. Trying to fix my ignorance was how I found the Lord and was well worth the time to do so.

Conclusion

We can see from what has been mentioned that your worldview is shaped by many different things that we may not even realise! What you believe is therefore limited by what you know.

The way you view and perceive the world affects everything you do, how you behave, and how you treat others. The world is constantly trying to push its message and agenda upon society daily. People are abandoning God at an alarming rate, either believing He does not exist, or we don't need Him anymore. If people believe they descended from animals, is it really any surprise when they behave like animals?

I have provided several reasons why the Earth cannot be old as claimed by many people of today, it mathematically does not work. Mathematics is God's language. Its use is found all over the universe. If you drop a book, you believe the law of gravity will pull it to the ground. That is the natural law in action and is a mathematical formula. Somewhat ironically the word universe is derived from two Latin words, *'uni'*, meaning singular and *'verse'* meaning a spoken sentence. We live in a single-spoken sentence...God said.

This book is here to help provide answers to some of the most common questions and objections to Christianity. It by no means can address every objection as we are just scratching the surface. We could delve very deep into many of these topics, with each one being a book on its own! I hope that this gives you enough knowledge to be confident in the scriptures to handle any day-to-day questions and at the same time be curious enough to investigate each of these separately in your own time, so you are better prepared to handle more in-depth conversations and be ready always to provide and answer questions for the hope that is within you. (Peter 3:15).

Chapter 4
Let's Get Controversial!

We are now going to get into controversial topics. Some of God's requirements seem unreal to us in a society constantly trying to push the world's narrative, as mentioned earlier, the details matter. God has different purposes for both the sexes and individuals. You do not buy a sports car if you want to drive cross country or across a farm, you buy an SUV or tractor. The design is different depending on its purpose yet all have propulsion and four wheels.

My daughter has a little stool she uses to reach the kitchen sink to wash her hands. One day she washed her hands and then moved her stool not even two feet away. When I came back into the room, I wasn't happy. She didn't understand why this was a problem, but she had placed her stool next to a burning gas hob with a red-hot metal saucepan containing boiling water as she wanted to help Dad stir her dinner! She did not understand why Dad did not want her in that position and that one false move could end badly.

God also has His reasons for putting in some unusual requirements, even if it doesn't seem a big deal to us. Remember if you get offended here, you need to ask God to examine your heart in prayer. Do not get attached to worldly things. We are in the world but not of the world. Do not get pride-filled as God will show favour to those willing to humble themselves. I also need to point out that as mentioned in Chapter 1, and mentioned in Matthew 5:17-18:

17 "Think not that I am come to destroy the law, or the prophets: I am not come to destroy, **but to fulfil.**

¹⁸ "For verily I say unto you, **Till heaven and earth pass, one jot or one tittle shall in no wise pass from the law, <u>till all be fulfilled</u>.**"

This also matters in parts of the law that many dispute or say are no longer relevant, we are under grace now. Yet nobody says committing murder or theft is okay now because we are now under grace! People dispute it because they don't like it. Jesus says not one jot or one tittle shall pass from the law until ALL be fulfilled. It is not yet all fulfilled...the law still applies, in many cases, Jesus ups the standard! When He is talking about the topic of adultery. In the olden days that meant 'doing' the act, Jesus says in Matthew 5:28:

²⁸ "But I say unto you, That whosoever looketh on a woman to lust after her hath committed adultery with her already in his heart."

In other words, if you think about it, you're guilty of it because the heart wants to sin. The question is do you believe what it says and trust Him enough that these requirements are for OUR benefit? Some things in the Bible will challenge us, we don't understand why it is there or seems like a daft requirement. But His ways are higher than ours. If we love Him, keep the commandments. With this in mind then let us continue.

Money

One area where most of the people I know, including me, have failed the Lord is with the subject of money and finances. It is such an important topic that 30% of the parables Jesus taught are on the very subject of money. I personally have often taken out loans or credit cards to pay for various things I wanted now and wasn't prepared to wait on the Lord to provide. Or even considered if He wanted me to have said item. When I reflect on my own life, God has always met my needs. Our needs and our WANTS are NOT the same thing.

Proverbs 22:7:

7 "The rich ruleth over the poor, And the borrower is servant to the lender."

Money is not inherently evil. The LOVE of it is. If God can trust you with a little, why wouldn't He give you a lot if He knows you can handle it and will use it to further His purposes? If you cannot be trusted with God's resources, He will not give you more. Most people would like to be rich, but then self-sabotage by telling themselves that money is evil. I mentioned in the introduction about the topic of prosperity being taught more than persecution. My observation comes from the fact that many teachers do not preach the parts of the Bible that make them uncomfortable. God does want us to prosper 100%. It is Satan who does not want you to because Satan knows that the rich rule over the poor. If true Christians become rich, we can have lasting impacts on the direction of the world. The devil doesn't want that. Jesus often discusses the topic of money. Remember the story of the talents in Matthew25: 14 – 30:

"For the kingdom of heaven is as a man travelling into a far country, who called his own servants, and delivered unto them his goods.

And unto one he gave five talents, to another two, and to another one; to every man according to his several ability; and straightway took his journey.

Then he that had received the five talents went and traded with the same, and made them other five talents.

And likewise he that had received two, he also gained other two.

But he that had received one went and digged in the earth, and hid his lord's money.

After a long time the lord of those servants cometh, and reckoneth with them.

And so he that had received five talents came and brought other five talents, saying, Lord, thou deliveredst unto me five talents: behold, I have gained beside them five talents more.

His lord said unto him, Well done, thou good and faithful servant: thou hast been faithful over a few things, I will make thee ruler over many things: enter thou into the joy of thy lord.

He also that had received two talents came and said, Lord, thou deliveredst unto me two talents: behold, I have gained two other talents beside them.

His lord said unto him, Well done, good and faithful servant; thou hast been faithful over a few things, I will make thee ruler over many things: enter thou into the joy of thy lord.

Then he which had received the one talent came and said, Lord, I knew thee that thou art an hard man, reaping where thou hast not sown, and gathering where thou hast not strawed:

And I was afraid, and went and hid thy talent in the earth: lo, there thou hast that is thine.

His lord answered and said unto him, Thou wicked and slothful servant, thou knewest that I reap where I sowed not, and gather where I have not strawed:

Thou oughtest therefore to have put my money to the exchangers, and then at my coming I should have received mine own with usury.

Take therefore the talent from him, and give it unto him which hath ten talents.

For unto every one that hath shall be given, and he shall have abundance: but from him that hath not shall be taken away even that which he hath.

And cast ye the unprofitable servant into outer darkness: there shall be weeping and gnashing of teeth."

In the parable, Jesus states that the one who hid it away is a vile and wicked servant. So, what did Jesus do? Did He apply the Robin Hood mentality of taking from the rich to give to the poor? No, He DID NOT take from the man who made ten, giving it to the one who only had one. He did the exact opposite, by taking the one talent and giving it to the man who had made it ten. At least he was going to do something with it. God will supply all your NEEDS according to HIS riches (Philippians 4:19). There are multiple meanings to this parable. The first as I'm sure many of you will be aware is that of souls. Each coin represents one soul saved. Those who share the gospel to win more souls for the Kingdom.

The other is in the concept of money itself. There is an old saying that to make money you must spend money. Investors are acutely aware of this. They do not invest hundreds, thousands, or millions of pounds/dollars to get no return. An example of this would be if a movie costs £10 million to make but brings in £100 million in revenue, that is a good return on investment.

In 1971 then US President Nixon took money off the gold standard. Cash used to be backed by silver and gold. But no longer. Now cash is a currency. A current, whether it be electrical or a water current, it needs to be constantly on the move. Otherwise, it stagnates. Savings get eaten up by inflation meaning it literally loses its purchasing power every year. Keeping large sums of money in the bank is a bad idea today. It needs to be moving. This is why the rich invest their money in the hope of greater returns.

The rich also use debt to obtain more assets and thus greater riches. It is often referred to as 'good' debt and 'bad' debt, with the 'good' debt being debt someone else pays for you. Richard Branson is on record as saying he aims to be the first man to die with 1 billion pounds worth of personal debt! He doesn't say that because he is stupid. He knows that that debt will make him richer. The masses are completely unaware of the difference between what is an asset versus a liability and I would highly advise you to educate yourself on how the financial system really works. It's an important topic.

But here's the thing. Rich people today use debt as a form of leverage. We have all used debt to acquire something. Our mortgage and or a car are the most common examples. The result is we now need to work a job that provides a certain salary to pay our lenders, and in turn, many of us give up on our dreams and God-given purpose to serve our lenders. Matthew 6:24 says you **CANNOT** serve two masters, for you will hate the one and love the other. So many of us go out and get ourselves a **Master** Card! Because we must serve a master. But what does the Bible teach about debt? What is God's way of handling money? The Bible makes it clear we are to lean on God to provide for our needs. Our earthly rules of money may have changed but God's way has not. Every mention of debt in the Bible is negative in content.

In Romans 13:8:

⁸ "Owe no man anything, but to love one another hath fulfilled the law."

It tells us we are to owe no man. It does not say you can owe one man something. Now this one is harder to work out and come to terms with. Most homeowners have a mortgage, becoming servants of the bank. This one is by far the biggest trap most of us fall into with buying a vehicle being in close second. If I fail to make these payments, then 'my' home can and will be repossessed. This is not trusting in the Lord and His provision. If it were, He would tell us to accept riches from the lenders. But why does God tell us to owe no man? The answer is actually pretty simple. God is our provider, not the bank or lender.

In Psalm 23:1:

¹ "The LORD is my shepherd; I shall not want."

Or in Philippians 4:19:

¹⁹ "But my God shall supply all your **need** according to **his** riches in glory **by** Christ Jesus."

Jesus taught us to have a budget! In Luke 14:28-30:

"For which of you, intending to build a tower, sitteth not down first, and counteth the cost, whether he have sufficient to finish it?

Lest haply, after he hath laid the foundation, and is not able to finish it, all that behold it begin to mock him,

Saying, This man began to build, and was not able to finish."

We must make sure we have enough of a budget to finish our intended projects and set a budget accordingly. A budget does not mean cheap. It means to set a figure and know where your money is going and not be wondering where it went! There is a prayer that nobody prays when it comes to the topic of money, it is found in Proverbs 30:7-9:

"Two things have I required of thee; deny me them not before I die:

Remove far from me vanity and lies: give me neither poverty nor riches; feed me with food convenient for me:

Lest I be full, and deny thee, and say, Who is the LORD? or lest I be poor, and steal, and take the name of my God in vain."

I don't know anyone who has prayed this. This prayer is asking God to give just enough for the day, so they do not forsake Him, many people in their riches think they do not need Him. We all say we want to be rich, yet many people who get money will often forget their need for God, and in all instances obtaining money before you are ready will only amplify your problems, not reduce them as many believe. In Revelation 3:17:

[17] "Because thou sayest, I am rich, and increased with goods, and have need of nothing; and knowest not that thou art wretched, and miserable, and poor, and blind, and naked"

Is God your provider? Or is it man?

Matthew 6:25:

[25] "Therefore I say unto you, Take no thought for your life, what ye shall eat, or what ye shall drink; nor yet for your body, what ye shall put on. Is not life more than meat, and the body than raiment?"

Matthew 6:33-34:

³³ "But **seek ye first the kingdom of God**, and his righteousness; and all these things shall be added unto you.

³⁴ Take therefore **no thought for the morrow**: for the morrow shall take thought for the things of itself. Sufficient unto the day is the evil thereof."

Matthew 7:7-11:

"Ask, and it shall be given you; seek, and ye shall find; knock, and it shall be opened unto you:

For every one that asketh receiveth; and he that seeketh findeth; and to him that knocketh it shall be opened.

Or what man is there of you, whom if his son ask bread, will he give him a stone?

Or if he ask a fish, will he give him a serpent?

If ye then, being evil, know how to give good gifts unto your children, how much more shall your Father which is in heaven give good things to them that ask him?"

I think God is trying to make it clear that we are to go to Him for our needs and to give to Caesar the things that are Caesar's, and to God, the things that are God's. (Matthew 22:21).

When the prophet Elijah was hidden for God to prepare him to fulfil his calling, he was by the brook of Cherith in 1 Kings17:4-6. God sent the ravens to feed him. This means God had to feed the ravens too.

When Moses led the people out of Egypt, God provided bread from heaven.

Exodus 16:4-5:

4"Then said the LORD unto Moses, Behold, I will rain bread from heaven for you: and the people shall go out and gather a certain rate every day, that I may prove them, whether they will walk in my law, or no."

5 And it shall come to pass, that on that sixth day- they shall prepare that which they bring in; and it shall be twice as much as they gather daily."

God will provide for his people, but we need to trust Him and His timing. Which often does not match our own and will not be when or how we expect it, but by listening to Him and doing what He asks, even when that seems strange and/or scary, which it often will. (This book is a result of me doing what He has asked).

I see so many people in society calling for taxing the rich. The tax the rich is a fool's errand. Nobody poor will ever offer you a job. Nobody poor will feed the hungry, not because they are unloving, or not generous, as He loves a cheerful giver, but it is very difficult to be generous when you are broke. Rich people are rich. They can afford to leave should the taxes get too high; they then take their jobs with them and the poor and middle class often pick up the tab. The very people who vote for these things will often end up footing the bill themselves. This happened famously when the Tesla Company left California and went to Texas and took all their jobs with them due to the constant increases in taxation. Followed by many other companies. The universal rules of abundance apply to everyone. God is our provider; God can also take away. The trap people fall into is trying to keep up with the Joneses by buying that new car you didn't need, or that phone upgrade when the old phone still runs the same operating system and works just fine, keeping you in debt and a slave to your lenders. The rich are productive to the point they need help to grow more, and in turn, create jobs to increase productivity.

The wealthiest people I have met are the ones who also give the most and some of the nicest. Funny how that is often overlooked. Society has been taught to hate the rich. Have some got their riches by ill-gotten gains or by exploiting others? Absolutely, but that is not the majority. If God has blessed you with great financial wealth, He hasn't done it so you can get that bigger house or nicer car, laying up treasures on earth where things rust. He has given you more so you can give and bless others more. If He can't trust you a little, how then can He give you more? He won't give you more than you can handle. It would be like giving a 1000-horsepower car to a 17-year-old who only just passed their test. Not smart.

Galatians 6:7-8:

"Be not deceived; God is not mocked: for whatsoever a man soweth, that shall he also reap.

For he that soweth to his flesh shall of the flesh reap corruption; but he that soweth to the Spirit shall of the Spirit reap life everlasting."

If you plant an apple seed, you expect to get an apple tree. Money is also used as seeds. You must plant it well if it is to work for you. You will reap what you sow, but that is true for all areas of your life, not just financial. Most people do not sow anything, and then wonder why they reap nothing. The sun will still shine, and the rain will still fall, but if you don't plant anything, you won't reap anything.

1 Corinthians 15:33:

³³ "Be not deceived: evil communications corrupt good manners."

You cannot hold two conflicting ideas in your mind, you will self-sabotage. It is known as cognitive dissonance. The reason so many struggle financially is that they are constantly listening to people who have negative financial patterns. You cannot become wealthy if you are constantly criticising people who are wealthy. Your mind will not tolerate it. You will become who you surround yourself with. We all know that we do not want our children to get involved with a bad crowd because that behaviour rubs off. If you want to get better at prayer, financial status, etcetera, then surround yourself with those who are better than you and you want to be like.

In Conclusion

In the story of the wealthy man in Matthew 19, the wealthy man goes to Jesus, "I have done all the commandments what do I lack?" Jesus then tells him to sell all his possessions and follow Him. This left the young wealthy man feeling sorrowful because he had great possessions. Notice Jesus didn't ask Peter or the other disciples to sell their possessions. Why did he ask this man to? The issue was who or what has you? The man went away sorrowful. The possessions owned his heart, not the Lord.

Having a lot of possessions or money is not sinful. It is where your heart is that is the problem and Jesus knew it. When I was out of work, I had the motorcycle I always wanted sleeping in the garage. I remember praying to the Lord asking Him that if selling it was required to stay on His path, so I could meet my financial commitments and that I would willingly sell it. Less than 24 hours after, I was offered a new job. I am certain that is because my heart was willing to surrender my possessions to follow the Lord if that was required of me. My NEED has always been met and I trust in Him to always meet that, do you trust Him to meet your needs? Just because our human ways of handling money have changed, God's way has not.

Health

This section will make some of you uncomfortable and will challenge some of your deeply held beliefs. I have no doubt I'll be accused of being a conspiracy theorist, so I urge you to go and do some of your own research. There is an old saying that seeing is believing. There are some things I do not need to see to believe in them, such as air and gravity. Many people who have challenged the beliefs of their time bring about some kind of hornets' nest when sharing their beliefs and challenging the status quo. I fully expect this topic to do the same.

'Those who are able to see beyond the shadows and lies of their culture will never be understood, let alone, believed, by the masses.' Plato

In Genesis 1:29 God tells Adam what he needs to eat:

[29] "And God said, Behold, I have given you every herb bearing seed, which is upon the face of all the earth, and every tree, in the which is the fruit of a tree yielding seed; to you it shall be for meat."

When God first made everything, all of creation only ate plants. It even says so in Genesis 1:30:

30 "And to **every beast** of the earth, and to **every fowl** of the air, and to **every thing** that creepeth upon the earth, wherein there is life, **I have given every green herb for meat**: and it was so."

We are to eat the green herbs, fruit-yielding seed, AND THE SEED. I don't know many people who sit there eating seeds. The number of people who die from eating herbs and vegetables is zero. How many people have died by taking drugs? God has provided EVERYTHING we need to sustain us and told us what to eat to remain functional.

In Psalm 104:14-15:

"He causeth the grass to grow for the cattle, **and herb for the service of man**: that he may bring forth food out of the earth;

15 And wine that maketh glad the heart of man, and oil to make his face to shine, and bread which strengtheneth man's heart."

In God's original design, every living creature ate plant life. Plants produce no blood and are not alive, it is our modern world that claims plants are 'alive'. It was only after the flood that God permitted eating meat, in Genesis 9:3:

3 "Every moving thing that liveth shall be meat for you; even as the green herb have I given you all things."

There are several reasons for this. First is that the once plentiful vegetation has been destroyed by the flood waters. Our planet is 70% surface water today. The water on the surface used to be under the surface. Second, everything you eat is somehow linked to a plant. We eat the cow, which eats the grass, and so on. However, in Leviticus, God tells the people of Israel there are some foods/meats you must not eat. When you go through it, you'll notice that the animals banned are those that tend to eat other animals and scavengers. These harbour the most parasites.

Wait but sharp teeth are for meat eaters, right?

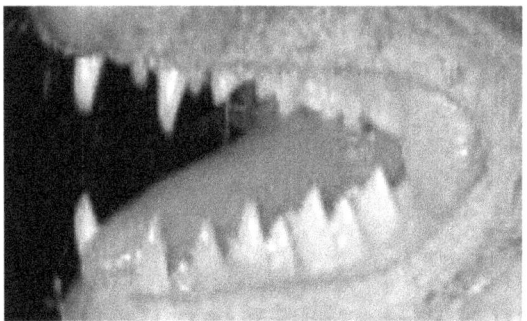

These are the teeth of a fruit bat. Only eats fruit.

Below is the skull of a Chinese water deer, a deer still wandering around, and has teeth like a sabretooth tiger! It doesn't eat meat either.

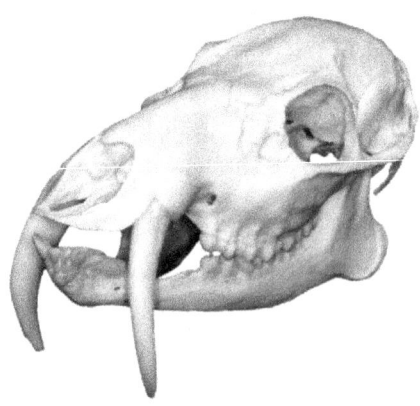

Having sharp teeth does not indicate they are meat eaters.

Peach and apricot seeds for instance contain B^{17}. Which is half cyanide. It is also found in apple seeds, bitter almonds, cherry seeds, and plum seeds, to name a few. But cyanide is poison, right? The cyanide is mixed with benzaldehyde, both separately are poisonous in the right doses, but not when combined. Then they are harmless until they encounter cancer cells. Now this of course is disputed and not approved as cancer treatment by the likes of the Food and Drug Administration (FDA) who claim the release of hydrogen cyanide in the body is potentially toxic. NOTE: Drug companies do not make money when you are firing on all cylinders.

Seeds cannot be regulated, drugs can though. Hydrogen, is highly explosive, so much so the sun runs on it, and oxygen, is also highly flammable, but mix them together, and you get water or H_2O. Which is both safe and essential for your survival, and most of your body is made up of that! Drink too much water though and you can be intoxicated from water poisoning and die from that too. Overdosing on anything will kill you. Sodium is poisonous, so is chlorine. Mix them though and you get salt. Which is great on almost everything.

The Hunza tribe of Northern Pakistan has never gotten cancer. One of their favourite foods happens to be apricot seeds. You don't get told that in medical school. All these drug and medicine companies do not make any money when you are completely well. A patient cured is a customer lost. The reality is that God has provided everything we need to prevent sickness if we just follow His instructions! Most illnesses and diseases are either a lack or excess of something. The Greek physician Hippocrates is quoted to have said:

'Disease always comes either from an excess of from a deficiency, that is, from an imbalance.'

It is still true today. The imbalance or excess of something makes you unwell. The more we move away from God's diet and more onto fast foods, carbonated drinks, etcetera, the more I predict we'll get more and more illnesses and health problems.

The British navy lost over a million sailors to an illness called scurvy. They cured scurvy by eating limes and they became known as 'the limies'. What they didn't know back then was about multivitamins and minerals contained within the limes, they just knew when you ate limes, you didn't get scurvy. What cured scurvy was none other than vitamin C. When they were at sea, often for months at a time, they were not getting enough vitamins and minerals which were in the fruits, green herbs, and seeds. Scurvy is caused by none other than a vitamin C deficiency. A lack of vitamin D is also the cause of a bone disease known as Ricketts.

Remember in Genesis God said to eat the green herb, fruit-yielding seed, and the seed thereof and herb for the **service of man** in Psalm 104:14-15. Do what God says. Eating what God tells you to eat is like having an oil change! What you eat will affect your mood and energy levels. You are what you eat as they say.

Motor manufacturers build systems into the vehicle such as the engine management light to alert you to a problem. You can ignore the problem if you want or fix it. My brother used to experience migraines as a child. The migraine wasn't the problem. It was the body warning him of a problem. If your body is hurting, or you are sick then pay attention! It's your body's warning system trying to tell you something. You can pop pills, but you are masking the real problem. Learn to listen to your body. Write down everything you eat and drink over a week and see how much of that is part of God's nutrition plan.

In Isaiah 38:5:

5 "Go, and say to Hezekiah, Thus saith the LORD, the God of David thy father, I have heard thy prayer, I have seen thy tears: behold, **I will add unto thy days fifteen years.**"

Hezekiah was the king of Judah. He had access to the best medical doctors and physicians of his time. However, he went straight to the throne room of God and as a result, God added 15 years to his lifespan. He went to God FIRST. Is prayer the FIRST thing you do when you are unwell? Do not misunderstand me. I'm not saying don't have headache tablets or visit doctors. I am saying, go to God first and understand why you have the headache or illness to start with. You may need a doctor to diagnose you, and you can go from there.

But here is an unpopular thought. If you have genuinely given your life to Christ and believe in God's Word, why are you scared of death? The biggest reason people go to the doctor in the first place is because they fear dying and are trying to preserve their own lives. Luke 9:23-24:

23 "And he said to them all, If any man will come after me, let him deny himself, and take up his cross daily, and follow me."

24 For whosoever will save his life shall lose it: but whosoever will lose his life for my sake, the same shall save it."

In Philippians 1:21:

21 "For to me to live is Christ, and to die is gain."

To die is GAIN? You get to go and be with the Lord in paradise if you have given yourself to Jesus, why would you be afraid of that? Maybe that trip to the doctor isn't to save you, you are saved already, but for you to witness and save them?

When the Covid pandemic came around in 2020 I refused to have the jab. I haven't had any jabs for quite a while. I didn't take it because God made me right the first time and He can heal me if He chooses to. If He chooses not to then maybe there is a reason for that. I want my faith to be like that of Job. I prayed and asked God to heal me and until I was healed, I would continue to seek His face regardless. I believed my prayer had been answered and expected it, I wanted the faith of Job. I didn't know why I felt the way I did but I prayed that I would take it and lean not on my understanding. Maybe God was not wanting me to ride my motorbike that week. Maybe Satan had asked God to put me down. I doubt that one but if he did, I'll take it as an honour he went to the trouble of asking permission! I haven't had Covid since even though many of my jabbed friends have had multiple jabs and had Covid multiple times.

I've had two since I was old enough to decide for myself, and before coming to faith. Now when it comes to the scriptures, the topic of health and sickness is dealt with often by Jesus. In fact, He says, "Oh ye of little faith" a lot. Many took the jab because they were threatened with losing their job, so they took it anyway. They put their faith in what the world was telling them, and not in God's Word. It's important to remember it isn't what the scriptures say that is the question. The question really is: DO YOU ACTUALLY BELIEVE WHAT IT SAYS? How strong is your faith in Him? Yes, God has given knowledge to people to do amazing things medically, such as operations while both asleep and pain-free. But is that to allow more time for the unbelievers to come to Him? God does not need any of these to heal us from our sicknesses:

Psalm 103:3:

³ "Who forgiveth all thine iniquities; **who healeth all thy diseases;**"

It says heals ALL your diseases. Not 50% or 99%. He can heal you if He chooses to. At some point though, we will all have our appointment with Him, and we won't be late for it! At some point, He won't heal you. For the wages of sin is death (Romans 6:23).

Matthew 4:23:

²³ "And Jesus went about all Galilee, teaching in their synagogues, and preaching the gospel of the kingdom, **and healing all manner of sickness and all manner of disease among the people.**"

Matthew 8:3:

³ "And Jesus put forth his hand, and touched him, saying, I will; be thou clean. **And immediately his leprosy was cleansed.**"

In this verse, all Jesus did was lay a hand on him to be healed.

Matthew 8:13:

¹³ "And Jesus said unto the centurion, **Go thy way; and as thou hast believed, so be it done unto thee. And his servant was healed in the selfsame hour.**"

In this verse, Jesus healed the servant who wasn't even present! Because you have believed, so it be done. He did make him wait an hour though.

Matthew 9:20-22:

"And, behold, a woman, which was diseased with an issue of blood twelve years, came behind him, and touched the hem of his garment

For she said within herself, If I may but touch his garment, I shall be whole.

But Jesus turned him about, and when he saw her, he said, **Daughter, be of good comfort; thy faith hath made thee whole. And the woman was made whole from that hour.**"

Her faith made her whole. She believed He could heal her, so He did so, again it was within that hour. What is your level of faith? God will not heal everything though. Otherwise, we'd all be living forever when the scripture teaches that death is a result of sin and none of us are sin-free.

Matthew 13:58:

[58] "**And he did not many mighty works there <u>because of their unbelief.</u>**"

Because of their unbelief, He didn't perform His works. Your belief in Him has a HUGE impact on the works you will see from Him. Many of those you will meet in church will attest to this.

Matthew 14:29-31:

[29] "And he said, Come. And when Peter was come down out of the ship, he walked on the water, to go to Jesus.

[30] But when he saw the wind boisterous, he was afraid; and beginning to sink, he cried, saying, Lord, save me.

31 And immediately Jesus stretched forth his hand, and caught him, and said unto him, **O thou of little faith, wherefore didst thou doubt?"**

Take this into consideration. Peter started to walk on the water! Once he realised what was going on he started sinking. When Jesus came to get him the first thing, He said was, "You have little faith, why did you doubt?" This was Peter, who had seen the mighty works of Jesus firsthand and still had doubts. It will be tough for us who have not seen, but blessed are those who have not seen, yet have believed (John 20:29).

Matthew 17:16-17:

"And I brought him to thy disciples, and they could not cure him.

Then Jesus answered and said, **O faithless and perverse generation, how long shall I be with you? how long shall I suffer you? bring him hither to me."**

The disciples could not cure him, whereupon Jesus then says they are, "both faithless and perverse. How long do I have to put up with you?" I won't always be with you, sort it out!

There is a common theme here. Your faith is what makes you whole. It doesn't say pop pills and medicines until it fixes the issue. I am not against them; they certainly help to remove pain from surgeries and assist with problems, but what I am saying is to understand what causes them, take them to God and deal with the root first. So many people give the universe mixed messages and then wonder why it doesn't come to fruition. They keep subconsciously asking for different things. You must make decisions for yourself, nobody else can make those choices for you. I'm a big believer that prevention is better than cure. But ultimately death will come for us all, as all have sinned, and we will not be late for our appointment with the Lord.

Climate Change

I hear the climate change and climate crisis constantly on the news and within my own circles about the world getting warmer and x number of degrees means this will happen etcetera. Firstly, nobody knows what will happen except the Lord, and second, the point of this book is whether you trust the Lord and His Word or not. Do you believe He is in control or not? Is God the one who controls the climate? If you said yes to these then what are you worried about? God said He will make a new heaven and a new Earth. You either believe that or you don't. If you do, you have nothing to concern yourself with. Remember, perfect love, casts out fear. If you are fearful of world events, you are still being made perfect in love. But the reality is you have nothing to fear, He hasn't given you a spirit of fear. In 2 Timothy 1:7:

7 "For God hath not given us the spirit of fear; but of power, and of love, and of a sound mind."

In 1 Corinthians 10:26:

26 "For the earth is the Lord's, and the fulness thereof."

People assume that carbon emissions are 100% the reason. What is not even considered is the fact the moon is slowly drifting away from the earth. The moon not only controls the tides but also keeps the earth at a stable 23° angle and it is believed that is what stops the earth from wobbling in space, almost acting like a balance shaft in an engine. What is the effect on the earth as it drifts even further away?

Let's use an engineering example, if we have a chain going around on a sprocket and we slowly remove that chain by a few millimetres per rotation, eventually the chain separates and the sprocket stops turning. Interesting how the earth's rotation speed is also slowing down then isn't it? The alarmists scream that a few degrees of temperature rise are catastrophic, so what about the few centimetres a year, the moon is moving? What about the sun's activity concerning sunspots and events on the surface? None of that is even considered in the equation.

There are also considerably more trees now than there were just a few hundred years ago, this is because we no longer cut them down to burn and keep warm in the winter months, and we use less paper in favour of screens. There are so many more variables at play and to suggest the burning of fossil fuels as 100% the cause is just ignorance. But maybe, just maybe, it is an effect of the earth's ageing process. We wear out as we age. The earth is doing the same. Hebrews 1:10-11:

"And, Thou, Lord, in the beginning hast laid the foundation of the earth; and the heavens are the works of thine hands

They shall perish; but thou remainest; and <u>they all shall wax old</u> as doth a garment;"

The Earth belongs to God. It does not belong to us. We are charged with tending it. You could argue we have done that poorly and I wouldn't argue about that. We currently live in a cause-and-effect world.

'For EVERY action there is an equal and opposite REACTION'.
Issac Newton

People have either forgotten or are ignorant of all the problems that modern vehicles and machinery solved. Think for a moment what would happen if we replaced cars and went back to horses. This creates several issues.

Horses eat and poop a lot. This means we need people to sweep up said faeces. Back in the day we didn't have enough people to shovel the poop which meant diseases, flies and if you don't like spiders, there would need to be more of those too! The environmental impact of waste management, feed, and methane emissions is considerable. Using horses would also require substantial maintenance as urban areas would need facilities for stables, feeding, and caring for the animals, which would take up considerable space. The cost of keeping live animals is also considerable. The only obvious positive I see is that the council won't need to cut the grass as often!

Huge productivity loss. Humans and animals are much slower than our machines. The whole point of many of these machines we made was to increase productivity.

Travelling any distance would take weeks or months. Good luck holding a job with any reasonable commute required. Emergency services would be considerably slower as would our lifestyle. Our 'world' would shrink considerably. Modern supply chains rely on speed and efficiency, switching that would lead to shortages and increased costs.

All that food we can just go and buy in the supermarket? Good luck getting it all there, not to mention how much extra land would be needed to breed and feed any animal we replaced machines with. Electric vehicles currently take hours to charge and still require fossil fuels to produce electricity. Yes, some of it is renewable but nowhere near enough to meet demand.

For all those activists out there preaching doom and gloom, screaming we must stop oil. Firstly, if we did that all modern society as we know it would collapse. Most moving parts need some form of lubrication. Oil happens to be one of the best. Second, if you do trust the Lord and know His word then you should know that when everything does get bad, oil isn't going anywhere. In Revelation 6:6:

6 "And I heard a voice in the midst of the four beasts say, A measure of wheat for a penny, and three measures of barley for a penny; **and see thou hurt not the oil and the wine.**"

Oil and wine are not going anywhere anytime soon. This statement in Revelation is the reason I bought shares in oil companies. According to God, they are safe until the Lord makes a new heaven and new Earth. I care more about deforestation than I do about driving petrol/gas vehicles, keeping our communities tidy and recycling what we can to avoid waste, as nobody wants to live in a pigsty until the Lord makes a new one and we go and be with the Lord. We as humans cannot save the planet, that thinking is giving us a God complex. The planet does NOT need saving. We sinners do and only God does that. Maybe put your trust in Him and His word instead. Global warming will 100% happen though regardless as a form of punishment. Just like the flood beforehand, the next major judgement will be by fire. In Revelation 16:8-9:

8 "And the fourth angel poured out his vial **upon the sun; and power was given unto him to scorch men with fire.**

9 **And men were scorched with great heat**, and blasphemed the name of God, which hath power over these plagues: and they repented not to give him glory."

These people are so stuck in their ways they still won't repent! But, even with that, if you are saved in Christ, this should not be a concern to you as He has already told you in advance what will happen.

The reason the world wants you to focus and scare you on saving the planet is to apply the communist manifesto, which the number one pledge is to abolish private property. But the Bible makes it clear that ownership is an important part of one's liberty.

You see it in 1 Kings 4:25:

25 "And Judah and Israel **dwelt safely, every man under his vine and under his fig tree**, from Dan even to Beersheba, all the days of Solomon."

Then in Proverbs 5:15:

15 "Drink waters out of **thine own cistern, and running waters out of thine own well.**"

1 Corinthians 3:17:

17 "Now the Lord is that Spirit: **and where the Spirit of the Lord is, there is liberty.**"

We keep hearing about things like forest fires being a result of climate change, and things heating up. Here is what they don't tell you. A sheet of paper has an ignition temperature of 233 degrees centigrade (451 Fahrenheit). This means that if you leave a sheet of paper lying around it will not ignite on its own until it reaches 233 degrees. No day on earth is that hot. So how do these fires start? A tree, leaf, or bush is thicker than a piece of paper and does not just catch fire.

These fires are a result of human behaviour and negligence. Hot embers from BBQs, arson, or litter such as glass amplify heat, which can reach such high temperatures thus causing ignition. A magnifying glass can reach those temperatures as the photons are narrowed to a localised area. It is NOT caused just because a particular day was 50 degrees. We might struggle in 50 degrees, but nature will not, God made it more robust than that! In Greece, in 2023 there were fires over the islands. When I went to Greece in 2024, all the green land that had been burned had returned after ten months. Didn't mention that in the media, did they?

The world wants you to do certain things and behave in a certain way, so you get distracted and stray from God's Word and His path. Climate change, as it is being sold to us is just another of these tools and distracts believers and non-believers alike from the signs of the times spoken of by Jesus. The people pushing this are mostly unbelievers who do not believe in a heaven and hell and would like nothing more than to exert authority over you by using deception and human wisdom which is foolishness to God.

1 Corinthians 3:19:

[19] "For the wisdom of this world is foolishness with God. For it is written, He taketh the wise in their own craftiness."

Some of these disasters we've seen in recent years are not climate change in the manner in which it has been taught. I wouldn't argue that the earth is changing. The real question is what is the cause? In the same way, a 70-year-old body doesn't work quite the same as a ten-year-old body, the same is true with the earth. It is wearing out, and a sign of the return of Jesus. Satan tries to twist God's Word to match his agenda and lead people astray. Climate change as we have been taught is to blind the masses to the signs of the return of Jesus Christ. God states in Revelation that He will make a new heaven and a new earth. The question is, do you believe and trust in the Lord that He is in fact in control? Do not worry about it. Keep your area and community clean and tidy but know that the Lord is in control. There is a plan, and it will be made new one day so do not worry about it! Jesus told us about these changes in the famous sermon on the Mount.

Matthew 24:8:

8 "And ye shall hear of wars and rumours of wars: **see that ye be not troubled**: for all these things must come to pass, but the end is not yet. For nation shall rise against nation, and kingdom against kingdom: and there shall be famines, and pestilences, and earthquakes, in divers places. All these are the beginning of sorrows."

There are a few things to point out here. Firstly, Jesus says, "Do not be troubled". He says this because there is a plan, the more you know about the plan the less you panic. We read in Isaiah 46:10 that He declares the end from the beginning. If you read your Bible, you know how the story ends. Secondly, there shall be famines, pestilences, and earthquakes in divers places. The word 'pestilence' is another word for a disease or large-scale calamity.

If you just look at the earthquakes on a day-to-day basis you will unlikely notice anything unusual but instead, look at charts over the last 100 years... You'll notice a sharp rise in both frequency and intensity. Don't take my word for it. Go and look for yourself. Jesus was telling the truth. But if you read your Bible, none of what is happening in the world today should be a surprise to you. It is Satan who is trying to keep you distracted by telling you the changes in the climate are all our fault. It distracts you from the signs and keeps you from trusting God's Word and instead believing in worldly wisdom. Satan wants to pull you down to hell with him. Just like the crabs in a bucket phenomenon.

God has told you in advance that the earth SHALL perish. The Word shall indicate intention, obligation, or inevitability. It is guaranteed. Jesus has told us that these are the beginning of sorrows and a sign of His return. He is likening these events to a woman in labour. As the labour progresses the pain increases in both frequency and intensity until the baby arrives. These are signs you should not fear, nor be troubled by. Everything should be falling into place if you have read the scriptures. These events will continue to increase in both frequency and intensity until the return of Jesus Himself. Trust in Him and look forward to it!

Jesus said as a sign of His coming there would be an increase in deception, wars, and rumours of wars, famines, persecutions, pestilences, people being lovers of money, earthquakes would increase, and the love of many would wax cold. Just look at what is going on in the world today. Climate change is the devil's counter to the signs of the Lord's return and the devil always tries to counterfeit what God's Word states.

Your Obedience

Those of us who have kids want our children to obey our instructions. We do this to protect them and prevent them from harming themselves. God does the same for us, even when it seems to make little sense. How big is God in your eyes? Do we obey His commands? If we love Him, we are to keep His commandments.

What if He told you how to dress?

1Timothy 2:9:

⁹ "In like manner also, that women adorn themselves in modest apparel, with shamefacedness and sobriety; not with broided hair, or gold, or pearls, or costly array;"

Dress modestly? Modestly dressed does not mean a skirt that goes all the way to the ankles.

What if he tells you about your haircut?

1 Corinthians 11:14-15:

Doth not even nature itself teach you, that, **if a man have long hair, it is a shame unto him?**

But if a woman have long hair, it is a glory to her: for her hair is given her for a covering."

If a man has long hair, it is a shame to him? Let that sink in. This one makes me question the many paintings we have of Jesus. One because of this verse and second because short hair for men was the way it was during Roman times and Judas had to single Him out, I am not convinced Jesus had long hair. Many women wear a headscarf as a covering, this verse clearly states that long hair is the covering. No headscarf is required.

Does He tell you how to communicate?

Ephesians 4:29:

²⁹ "Let no corrupt communication proceed out of your mouth, but that which is good to the use of edifying, that it may minister grace unto the hearers."

Jesus himself says in Matthew 12:36-37:

"But I say unto you, **That every idle word that men shall speak, they shall give account thereof in the day of judgment.**

For by thy words thou shalt be justified, and by thy words thou shalt be condemned."

Don't swear, curse, or utter a profanity. Jesus says we are going to be held to account for every idle word that has left our lips! For what the mouth speaks, the heart is full of! Our speech should be that of love, grace, and truth. The truth can sting a bit though!

Does He tell you what you should / shouldn't watch and listen to?

Psalm 101:3:

³ "I will set **no wicked thing** before mine eyes: I hate the work of them that turn aside; it shall not cleave to me."

Ephesians 5:19

¹⁹ "Speaking to yourselves in psalms and hymns and spiritual songs, singing and making melody in your heart to the Lord;"

Distance yourself from evil. You shall put no wicked thing in your sight. It does not say you can put some wicked things before your eyes. It says **no wicked thing** in Psalm 101:3.

Do you put wicked things in front of your eyes? Movies where violence, murder, sex, etcetera are all glorified? The Bible warns against that, as it feeds your soul and makes you less attentive towards God. Almost every movie has a degree of violence, sexual immorality, or some other kind of sinful behaviour. It is in mainstream songs, and rap songs that glorify all kinds of wicked things. Some songs are hard to avoid, a lot of high street shops, carnivals, and festivals play them while you are out and about. It's hard to avoid and I have fallen into these traps. All you can do sometimes is pray to the Lord asking for protection and wear the full armour of God.

But we can't get around the fact we have been desensitised against wicked things. We now live in a time where good is called evil and evil is called good. Where homosexuality and transgenderism are openly celebrated and glorified. Homosexuality is openly condemned in pretty much every single religious text and is one of the very few things called an abomination to God. Do yourself a favour and avoid these things as much as you are able. You will become what you consume. The old saying, show me your friends and I will show you your future rings true here. The people you surround yourself with, the music and movies you watch all have an impact on how you conduct yourself in the world. Be mindful of that and pray on it regularly. There is a reason the Bible says to put no wicked thing in front of your eyes. The eyes are the windows to your soul.

Matthew 6:22-23:

[22] "The light of the body is the eye: if therefore thine eye be single, thy whole body shall be full of light.

23 "But if thine eye be evil, thy whole body shall be full of darkness. If therefore the light that is in thee be darkness, how great is that darkness!"

What you place in front of your eyes affects you. If you have a castle with a moat and a huge stone wall, the weak point is the gate where the entire castle can be taken over. You guard that gate to stop an opposing force. The importance of 'guarding your eyes' cannot be overstated. In Job 31:1-4, Job made a covenant with his eyes, there was a reason he did so! I remember playing a violent video game and this scripture came to mind and I had to turn the game off. It was at this moment I realised what being born again really meant. If you still indulge in these behaviours while claiming to be a Christian, you are not born again.

You cannot walk into a store without hearing certain music or turn on the TV without seeing something unholy. But you have dominion in your own home. What we do in private highlights our own spiritual state. Are you doing things in private that you know you should not be?

Sinful behaviour is all over our world now. Good is seen as evil and evil good. Just as the Bible predicts in Isaiah 5:20:

20 "Woe unto them that call evil good, and good evil; that put darkness for light, and light for darkness; that put bitter for sweet, and sweet for bitter!"

Just look at the society around you. Satan is no longer hiding his agenda, are you prepared for that? There was a time when you didn't need to lock your house. You'd leave your keys in the car, so you didn't lose them. You would be out of your mind to do that today. The very fabric of society is breaking. Once prayer was taken out of the schools, every metric deemed undesirable in society increased, from teenage pregnancy to murders, to suicide rates.

We as Christians are meant to be different. We are meant to be children of the light. The world is dark because people are not spreading the light. Light is constantly on the move. It is darkness that doesn't move. Do something for the Kingdom of God. We are not meant to have massive megachurches. We are required to make disciples and send them out further the Kingdom. If we don't do that Satan will do it to further his kingdom, which he is doing through music, media, culture, etcetera. If you are not a preacher, support the one who does preach. If you have lots of time, give some of it to spread the Gospel, and maybe write a book yourself about how God came to you and/or blessed you. If you are financially blessed, give some away, you cannot out give God and it is all His anyway. We can all do something for God and this is what we are called to do in Matthew 28:19-20:

[19] "Go ye therefore, and teach all nations, baptizing them in the name of the Father, and of the Son, and of the Holy Ghost"

[20] Teaching them to observe all things whatsoever I have commanded you: and, lo, I am with you always, even unto the end of the world. Amen."

In everything give thanks. Approach God with thanks. Make your requests known to God. Thankfulness can shift your mind and should be your habit.

James 1:22:

²² "Be ye doers of the word, and not hearers only, **deceiving your own selves.**"

In my journey, if I had known the full picture, I would have quit at the start. If you had told me when I was 18, I would be writing a book on truly trusting the Lord I would have laughed in your face as I didn't believe in God at all then, yet here I am.

Some of you would have experienced some incredible injustices, many at the hands of others, if that's you, you have my deepest sympathies. Take your experiences to prayer. He can heal you and in time you can forgive those who wronged you. There is an incredible power for those who can forgive, as I have experienced first-hand.

When it comes to forgiveness this is something we absolutely must do as Christians and that is one of the most difficult things to do. It is really important to highlight what Jesus said about this topic in Matthew 6:14-15:

"For if ye forgive men their trespasses, your heavenly Father will also forgive you

But if ye forgive not men their trespasses, neither will your Father forgive your trespasses."

We cannot have forgiveness from God unless we are willing to give it out ourselves. This is one of the most radical Christian beliefs and is paramount. This is because we have all sinned and broken the Lord's commandments, thus we are all worthy of His judgement. We often seek revenge. How many movies are based on that? I promise you that from experience being unwilling to forgive is willingly drinking from a poisoned chalice and is ill-advised. The only one getting hurt in that scenario is us. When Jesus was hanging on the cross, not once did he curse or seek revenge. Crucifixion was deliberately designed to be the most humiliating and painful death ever invented. And what did Jesus do? Forgave his torturers and murderers. "Forgive them, for they know not what they do."

What about commands that make us uncomfortable?

In Deuteronomy 22:28-29:

28 "If a man find a damsel that is a virgin, which is not betrothed, and lay hold on her, and lie with her, and they be found;

29 Then the man that lay with her shall give unto the damsel's father fifty shekels of silver, and she shall be his wife; because he hath humbled her, he may not put her away all his days."

I've been challenged on this one. The challenger implied that if a man were to rape a woman she is to be 'sold' off to the one who did the act. This is NOT what these verses are saying. The word 'betrothed' is another word for engagement, which shows a woman, the intent to marry her. These verses state that if a man and woman have sexual relations and they are not engaged, then he is required to marry her and commit to her for the rest of his life. It used to be very common in England that if you got an unmarried woman pregnant, you were required to marry her.

What they are trying to imply comes from the previous verses in Deuteronomy 22: 22-26:

22 "If a man be found lying with a woman married to an husband, then they shall both of them die, both the man that lay with the woman, and the woman: so shalt thou put away evil from Israel.

²³ If a damsel that is a virgin be betrothed unto an husband, and a man find her in the city, and lie with her;

²⁴ Then ye shall bring them both out unto the gate of that city, and ye shall stone them with stones that they die; the damsel, because she cried not, being in the city; and the man, because he hath humbled his neighbour's wife: so thou shalt put away evil from among you.

²⁵ If a man find a betrothed damsel in the field, and the man force her, and lie with her: then the man only that lay with her shall die.

²⁶ But unto the damsel thou shalt do nothing; there is in the damsel no sin worthy of death: for as when a man riseth against his neighbour, and slayeth him, even so is this matter"

In verse 25 it states if the man forces her, then only he shall die for there is no sin in her worthy of death. But if they are engaged and commit adultery, they are both to be stoned, as it is considered evil. The chances of that happening though were slim. Jesus himself demonstrated this when confronted with the woman caught in adultery with the famous line in John 8:7:

⁷ "He who is sinless among you, shall cast the first stone."

Which, they all up and left because they knew they were hypocritical. Jesus knew the law, yet none of them have kept it so have no right to execute judgement on things they themselves are guilty of. According to the Bible, sin is the very reason we experience death in the first place. For the wages of sin, is death (Romans 6:23). Critics do not like the idea of death and judgement for their actions which is why they criticise. Sexually transmitted diseases are everywhere today because we rebel against this and want to have multiple partners.

Another one that will come up is found in Numbers 31:17-18:

¹⁷ "Now therefore kill every male among the little ones, and kill every woman that hath known man by lying with him.

¹⁸ But all the women children, that have not known a man by lying with him, keep alive for yourselves."

See God is evil because He tells the Israelites to kill men and children while keeping the virgins as sex slaves! Firstly, it does not tell them to keep sex slaves, just the virgins. Like it or not God's original design is for us to stay pure until we are married and stay with that one. Second, they also miss out on the verse before these, in Numbers 31:16:

¹⁶ "Behold, these caused the children of Israel, through the counsel of Balaam, to commit trespass against the Lord in the matter of Peor, and there was a plague among the congregation of the Lord."

In the verse before it states there was a plague among them. It does not specify what kind of plague. Balaam was a prophet summoned by Balak, the king of Moab, to curse Israel but instead, he ended up blessing them. Despite this, Balaam contributes to Israel's downfall by advising Balak to seduce the Israelites into idolatry and sexual immorality. This plague was only stopped when the grandson of Aaron, takes a spear and kills an Israelite man and Midianite woman engaging in idolatrous practices.

There is every reason to suspect this plague was of a sexual nature and God wanted it removed and the command to kill them is part of the judgement against the Midianites for their role in leading Israel into idolatry and immorality, while also removing the future threats of military opposition. Many will not like that answer, but Numbers 31:17 reflects a complex interplay of justice and judgement. God will bring justice and judgement to those who sin against Him, this includes the Israelites themselves, which God has done many times. In the time of Jeremiah, the Israelites were constantly persistent in their idolatry and disobedience, leading to the prophet delivering a message from God that was very difficult for the people of Judah to accept. He repeatedly warned the people, including King Zedekiah, that they should not resist the Babylonian invasion, but surrender.

Jeremiah's prophecies emphasized that this invasion was God's judgement on Judah. He urged them to surrender to save their lives and prevent the destruction of the city. Of course, this message was extremely unpopular, as God's messages often are, especially among the leaders and commanders who saw this as treasonous, while in reality, these leaders were apostates. As a result, Jeremiah was persecuted, imprisoned, and threatened with death. Despite the opposition, Jeremiah remained steadfast in his warnings, insisting that surrendering to the Babylonians was the only way to preserve life, while resistance would lead to certain destruction.

Unfortunately, King Zedekiah and the people of Judah did not heed the warnings, and they chose to resist, which led to the siege and eventual destruction of Jerusalem, the burning of the temple, and the exile of the survivors to Babylon, including the prophet, Daniel. By ignoring the warning, they lost on both fronts.

Identity, Sexual Immorality and Transgenderism

2 Timothy 3:16-17:

2 "**All scripture** is given by inspiration of God, and is profitable for doctrine, for reproof, for correction, for instruction in righteousness:

2 That the man of God may be perfect, thoroughly furnished unto all good works."

1 John 2: 15-17:

¹⁵ "Love not the world, neither the things that are in the world. If any man love the world, the love of the Father is not in him.

¹⁶ For all that is in the world, the lust of the flesh, and the lust of the eyes, and the pride of life, is not of the Father, but is of the world.

¹⁷ And the world passeth away, and the lust thereof: **but he that doeth the will of God abideth for ever.**"

One of the first things Satan was to get Eve to question her God-given identity and one area where Satan is still hard at work is to attack our identity and break down the family unit. This is one of the most attacked areas of our faith today and something we as Christians are to rebuke. Suggesting that people are fine as we are, just be you. If you do that then, hell is where you will end up, lying to people is not loving. Telling the truth is. Our identity as a nation and as individuals is becoming an increasing problem.

Most recently in England, we had the Brexit referendum, which I voted for. One of the main reasons I did so was the basis that God deliberately split up the nations and mixed up our languages. The reason He did this was because when we were building the tower of Babel to the heavens, thus trying to put ourselves on God's level. We were all of one language and could achieve amazing things. But we are evil. Imagine the evil that could be done if we got that big. Unified sinners only bring hell. To prevent that happening God had to intervene. The result is that the nation-state is our safeguard against tyranny and evil rule and will remain so until we go back to the Lord. One area Satan has been working hard on as a result is the idea of globalisation, which is required for the anti-Christ and mark- of-the-beast system to come to fruition, which we'll cover later. God divided us into Nations to prevent this level of evil from taking over the world and I want to prevent that as long as possible. Yes, it will still happen anyway, but I'd rather delay it as much as possible. God delayed His judgement when the people of Nineveh repented after Jonah preached to the people.

The family unit is one of those things coming under constant attack now, under the guise of equality. This is because the feminists want to be done with the 'patriarchy'. A lot of this supposed outrage is simply rebellion against God. Men and women have been wired differently by our creator and as such we both have strengths and weaknesses in different areas and are more prone to lean towards a certain career type. Women tend to be more nurturing, which is why they are more prominent in nursing and teaching, while men are more geared more toward engineering and the trades etcetera. Under the Juneau Christian foundation, Western societies have flourished as both sexes have understood each other's strengths and weaknesses and played on that. Our modern society however is trying to destroy the very foundation which built modern society. Jesus himself said in Mark 3:24-25:

"And if a kingdom be divided against itself, that kingdom cannot stand.

And if a house be divided against itself, that house cannot stand."

The woman was made to be a help mate for the man. Not the other way around. I'm not against men and women having careers in any field, but what society doesn't tell women is at some point in their life the chance of them desiring a child is very likely. For humans, conception is quite difficult. As women age the chances of conception go down. This is most notable after the age of 35 and even harder post 40. An issue that does not affect men.

In Ephesians 5:22:

"Wives, submit yourselves unto your own husbands, as unto the Lord."

It says to submit to your husbands; it doesn't say submit to every man. As the husband is to submit to Christ. It also does not say husbands and husbands or wives and wives. Just by saying this, you'll come to blows with society. Well, friendship with the world is enmity with God anyway. God made us male and female for a reason. Verse 23:

"For the husband is the head of the wife, even as Christ is the head of the church: and he is the saviour of the body."

Part of the curse, and it is a curse for both, is women should submit to their husbands and men must love their wives as Christ loved the church in verse 25. Christ gave himself to the church. A man must give himself to his wife also. There is a divine order contained in marriage. Something society is so desperately trying to break down. The culture is trying to teach that patriarchy is evil when in reality it is God's defined order. Even Christians now try and squirm away from what it says to try and fit in with society. The argument made for not following this is that now we are in Christ, this male leadership does not apply, and the curse has been made void. Yet in Genesis 3:16, God says He will "greatly multiply thy sorrow and thy conception". In other words, it's going to hurt. Last time I checked, childbearing still hurts. It has not been reversed.

Adam was made first and the woman FOR the man as a helpmate and even formed out of Adam's rib and taken out of man in Genesis 2:21-

25. People hate male leadership because it is ordained by God and society today hates God. Those people are in rebellion against Him. It has nothing to do with our intrinsic value and everything to do with order. In much the same way the military has a chain of command, businesses have CEO's and organisational structures. Without it, everything becomes chaos. This rebellion is becoming increasingly apparent in society and the churches and is known as the Jezebel spirit and every church today has a Jezebel spirit in it. Both sexes have equal value, Adam says as much when he first sees Eve – "This is the flesh of my flesh, bones of my bones, she shall be called woman because she was taken out of man."

How many wives did God make for Adam? ONE. He did not make four, and he didn't make him another husband. Many texts throughout history condemn homosexuality. Just because we can do something, it doesn't mean we should. God has not ordained us to reproduce in that way. Ironically, they call it pride. Pride always comes before a fall. Sooner or later God will have no option but to judge this behaviour as He did with Sodom and Gomorrah. Whether you believe in God or believe it all came together by chance, neither option allows for two women or two men to naturally conceive a child. There is a reason for this, in much the same way two north sides of a magnet will not stick together, the fundamental laws of nature do not allow for some things.

Even if you believe in evolution, being homosexual is not an advantage. You aren't passing on your genes to anyone. Rebelling against this one is a fool's errand. Homosexuality is one of the few things God calls an abomination and a big contributor to why Sodom and Gomorrah were destroyed in the book of Genesis. Your chances of obtaining STDs increase considerably with same-sex and multiple partners. If I chose to have sex with any woman other than my wife, that would be deemed as sexual immorality. There is a reason we feel hurt and broken when have been cheated on. It is because we were designed to stick together and become one flesh. We were not supposed to have multiple sexual partners. If all we did was stay virgins until we married and then stay faithful to that one, how many sexual diseases would there be? Like none.

Even the well-known religious leaders are on record for blessing same-sex marriage. It should not be. No one can bless something God Himself, would not. The only marriage God recognises is between one man and one woman. I hear and see a lot of; love is love, but no it isn't. One of the most loving things I say to my children, besides I love you, is NO. Don't do that. Because I really do love and care about them, and I can see something that will hurt and damage them or someone else long before they can. Christians are meant to show love towards others. Christians are to love your neighbour as ourselves, and to even love our enemies! Love is how Christians are supposed to be easily identified. It holds no records of wrongs, love fulfils the law and my favourite, perfect love casts out fear.

But the word love has been abused. The most quoted verse in the whole Bible is that of John 3:16 where God so loved the world, He gave his only begotten son. It says God loved the world; it tells us not to love the world. The word 'world' has three meanings - the creation, the things in the world and the systems that make up the world. In simple terms love CAN be sinful. If I as a married man then love another and act on that, I'm committing a multitude of sins, including idolatry and adultery. So, what makes love sinful?

When it is aimed at the wrong thing and direction. Do not love the world nor the things in the world. What the world means in this context is the worldly things that are against God and his Word. The world is under the rule of Satan and not God's Kingdom. Much like the story of the rich man asked to sell his possessions mentioned earlier. He loved his things more than the Lord.

He who wants to be friends with the world makes himself an enemy of God and you cannot serve two masters. You'll love the one and hate the other. Loving the world is by default hating God. Christians have been chosen OUT of the world and the world hates you for it. (John 15:19)

Loving anyone other than your husband or wife. The one to whom you made your vows.

Love when it comes from the wrong source. As mentioned in verse 16 above, the lust of the eyes, **pride of life**, IS NOT FROM THE FATHER, BUT FROM THE WORLD. This lust and pride aren't coming from God. Lusts, and cravings all come from the world. Not from God.

Worshipping and serving the creature more than the creator (Romans 1:25).

When it produces the wrong fruit. Every tree that doesn't produce good fruit is hewn down (Matthew 7:19), implying that some do not produce good fruit.

Same-sex marriage is not from God and is not considered a marriage in His eyes. It is love that is aimed at the wrong thing and comes from the wrong source. They also cannot produce any fruit. By their unrighteousness, they suppress the truth.

Romans 1:18-24:

"For the wrath of God is revealed from heaven against all ungodliness and unrighteousness of men, who hold the truth in unrighteousness;

Because that which may be known of God is manifest in them; for God hath shewed it unto them.

For the invisible things of him from the creation of the world are clearly seen, being understood by the things that are made, even his eternal power and Godhead; <u>so that they are without excuse:</u>

Because that, when they knew God, they glorified him not as God, neither were thankful; but became vain in their imaginations, and their foolish heart was darkened.

Professing themselves to be wise, they became fools,

And changed the glory of the uncorruptible God into an image made like to corruptible man, and to birds, and fourfooted beasts, and creeping things.

Wherefore God also gave them up to uncleanness through the lusts of their own hearts, to dishonour their own bodies between themselves"

It does not bring any glory to the creator. Why would people even want to get married if they are not believers anyway? It is meant to be for a man and a woman to make their vows before the Lord. Why would you want to do that if you didn't believe it? Again, it boils down to man's rebellion. Even many unbelievers have a desire to get married, it's like they instinctively know it is meant to be that way. It also says God gave them up. The desires themselves are unholy. We do not tell married men and women to embrace their desires and cheat away, do we? Nobody thinks it is ok for a 40-year-old to be in 'love' with a minor. All of that is called out for what it is. As a Christian, I will pray for these people, and treat them the same but we cannot however endorse sinful and lust-filled passions. It is because we love them that we should tell them where these lusts will lead them. Romans 1:26-27:

²⁶ "For this cause **God gave them up** unto vile affections: for even their women did change the natural use into that which is **against nature**:

²⁷ And likewise also the men, **leaving the natural use of the woman**, burned in their lust one toward another; men with men working that which is unseemly, and **receiving in themselves that recompense of their error which was meet.**"

There is a shocking acceptance of these sins in society today, even among the Christian communities and it is this tolerance of these things that has allowed evil to flourish and even be glorified through worship and it must stop! There are some things Jesus Himself does not, and will not tolerate. Doing evil in the house of the Lord, He overturned the tables and called them a den of thieves in Matthew 21:12-13. You do not casually turn a table over. He threw it over.

From an engineering standpoint when something is made, we make it clear only to use something for its intended purpose and will not be liable for damages should said item be misused. You do not put diesel in a petrol engine, it will not run. But this 'fight' for equality is having undesired outcomes where men no longer feel the need to protect the physically weaker female. Where men who compete in sports in the mid-pack, transition to being a 'woman' and destroy the competition.

Sexual relations are very intimate. We all remember our sexual encounters, whether we realise it or not we link our souls to one another. There is a reason we become 'one flesh'. Sex is given a unique place when it comes to sin and how it impacts us. In 1 Corinthians 6:18:

18 "Flee fornication. Every sin that a man doeth is without the body; **but he that committeth fornication sinneth <u>against</u> his own body."**

We need to resist sexual immorality. This verse suggests that every other sin we commit is outside the body, but sexual sin against their own body. It indicates that sexual sin is unique and doesn't just affect the soul, but the body too, and carries uniquely earthly consequences, such as STDs, pregnancy, and murder of the innocent. Although all sin is equal in the sense of separation from God, there are distinctions based on those consequences, and harmful to us as individuals in the earthly realm. Watching unholy things on the internet harms your soul and impacts any relationship you have or could have had.

In the beginning, God made them 'male and female'. We inhibit a physical body. Spirits do not. Transgenderism is an attack by Satan to confuse people by getting them to think that they are not made in God's image. He pulled the same trick with Eve in the garden by suggesting God was withholding something from her, the knowledge of good and evil. Whatever God makes, Satan tries to counterfeit. If God made someone male, and they say I feel like a female, God did not make the mistake, they did. It is a spiritual attack that must be rebuked and repented of. Deuteronomy 22:5:

5 **"The woman shall not wear that which pertaineth unto a man, neither shall a man put on a woman's garment: <u>for all that do so are abomination</u> unto the LORD thy God."**

Wearing clothes pertaining to the opposite sex is one of the few things called an abomination to the

Lord, just like homosexuality. This is because it is directly against God's order and our identity in God's image. As a former atheist, I once accepted worldly things. But since asking the Holy Spirit to change me and give me the eyes to see and ears to hear, I have switched allegiances and now see the world for what it currently is, evil. You'll notice that once you do obey God instead, many if not all your old friends will leave because they are still in love with the world. If you have been born again, you have overcome the world. I'm not ashamed of God's Word, His creation, and divine order and neither should you be. Proclaim it boldly. Pray for those who are lost to come back fully to the Lord. Nobody is beyond saving, yet.

Abortion

Society hates kids so much they murder them in the womb. Those of us old enough, will remember the attacks on September 11th 2001, when there was a terrorist attack on the Trade Centre in America where 3000 people lost their lives. America spent millions of dollars trying to bring those responsible to justice. However, the day before another 3000 were murdered, and the day after that, and the day after that, in abortion clinics all around the country and nobody did anything. There is a 9/11 type of tragedy every day in the US alone. The argument is that it is just a foetus, it's just a clump of cells. This has the logic of 'guns kill people', no it's just a clump of metal and cutlery makes people fat. In all instances, they are the results of people making decisions. Abortion is the modern day child sacrifice.

The heartbeat starts in 3 weeks and 1 day. Is it ok to kill it then? Have you noticed that if a baby is aborted, they say foetus, but if a woman who is pregnant is murdered, the prosecutors say the woman and her 'unborn child'. This is because they can get a longer jail term for a double murder, so which is it? It's an unborn child when it suits. One of the things the Lord God hates is the shedding of innocent blood (Proverbs 6:16-19). It is murder, pure and simple, and all those going around even trying to justify it to themselves will have to account for EVERY idle word in the Day of Judgement mentioned in Matthew 12:36.

I've also heard that the baby cannot fend for itself. Neither can 100% of adults. How many of you built your house while out hunting for food, building materials, and water while healing any injuries and sickness along the way? The reality is that we are all dependent on others in some capacity for something. Nobody would last long solo in a desert environment. What about those who need around-the-clock care? How about we abort them too then? Survival of the fittest and all that? For, anyone to claim they are independent is simply in complete ignorance on their part, society has allowed people to think they are. Even for Adam and Eve, God had provided everything for them, ready to go.

My body, my choice. No, sounds like they want to abort someone else's body. All the people for abortion, interestingly have already been born, isn't it? I also hear the babies are unwanted. Children are the result of a man and woman having intercourse. Seed and egg. Two people made a decision, and there are consequences to every decision we make. If anyone is willing to abort a child because they are 'inconvenient', 'unwanted' or any other reason for that matter, that's a warning to you that these people cannot be trusted. Just as many babies being aborted are wanted by those who cannot have kids. The babies are not unwanted. God made the earth to be inhabited (Isaiah 45:18) and was the reason he made it.

The easiest way to not have kids is to not engage in the act or take other precautions. But do not justify murder to yourself because who knows what else could be 'justified' just to escape the consequences of poor actions and decision-making. God loves you and God can and will forgive you if you repent, but we must not justify it and pray for those even considering it.

Work

There are now some families with generations that haven't worked because society has allowed it.

I'm not against those in genuine need, but many people who could work are choosing not to. Considered benefits in the UK or welfare if you are in the USA. Since the fall, Gods benefits program is, you don't work, you don't eat as read in 2 Thessalonians 3:10-12:

10 "For even when we were with you, this we commanded you, **that if any would not work, neither should he eat.**

11 For we hear that there are some which walk among you disorderly, working not at all, but are busybodies.

12 Now them that are such we command and exhort by our Lord Jesus Christ, that with quietness they work, and eat their own bread."

Most people do not realise that laziness or idleness is considered sinful in the Bible. This all started in Genesis 3:17:

17 "And unto Adam he said, Because thou hast hearkened unto the voice of thy wife, and hast eaten of the tree, of which I commanded thee, saying, Thou shalt not eat of it: cursed is the ground for thy sake; in sorrow shalt thou eat of it all the days of thy life;"

God is telling Adam, that now you need to work for your food. I've cursed the ground, for your own good. This was not required before the fall. Manual labour is actually quite rewarding. I do not get the same satisfaction from producing a spreadsheet! But laziness is condemned in these passages:

Proverbs 10:4-5:

"He becometh poor that dealeth with a slack hand: but the hand of the diligent maketh rich.

He that gathereth in summer is a wise son: but he that sleepeth in harvest is a son that causeth shame."

Proverbs 12:24:

"The hand of the diligent shall bear rule: but the slothful shall be under tribute."

Proverbs 21:25-26:

"The desire of the slothful killeth him; for his hands refuse to labour.

He coveteth greedily all the day long: but the righteous giveth and spareth not."

These are just a handful of passages that condemn laziness. You can find more in, Proverbs 6:6-11, Proverbs 13:4, Proverbs 19:15, Proverbs 20:4, Ecclesiastes 10:18, Matthew 25:26-30, Romans 12:11, and Hebrews 6:12. The Bible consistently condemns laziness and promotes diligence, hard work, and responsibility. These passages highlight the negative consequences of being slothful and the value of industriousness, encouraging believers to be active and diligent in their daily lives and spiritual practices. Have you allowed yourself to become lazy?

The Light

One of the things the Bible describes God as is, he is the light thereof, in Revelation 21:23:

[23] "And the city had no need of the sun, neither of the moon, to shine in it: for the glory of God did lighten it, and the Lamb is the light thereof."

God is also described as omnipresent meaning he is always present everywhere. Satan does not share that same attribute, however. It describes God as the light thereof. Let's think about that. We as humans only see what we call visible light. God made two lights, one for the day and the lesser light to rule the night, as mentioned in Genesis 1. But that is only a small part of a large spectrum. X-rays, gamma rays, micro and radio waves are all part of a wider spectrum. The electromagnetic spectrum.

In the last 26 verses of the Bible, there is light but no sun. A lot of ancient cultures worship the sun. It is where Sunday comes from.

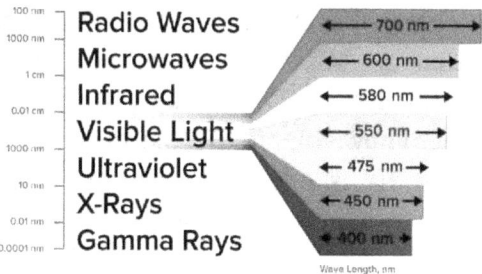

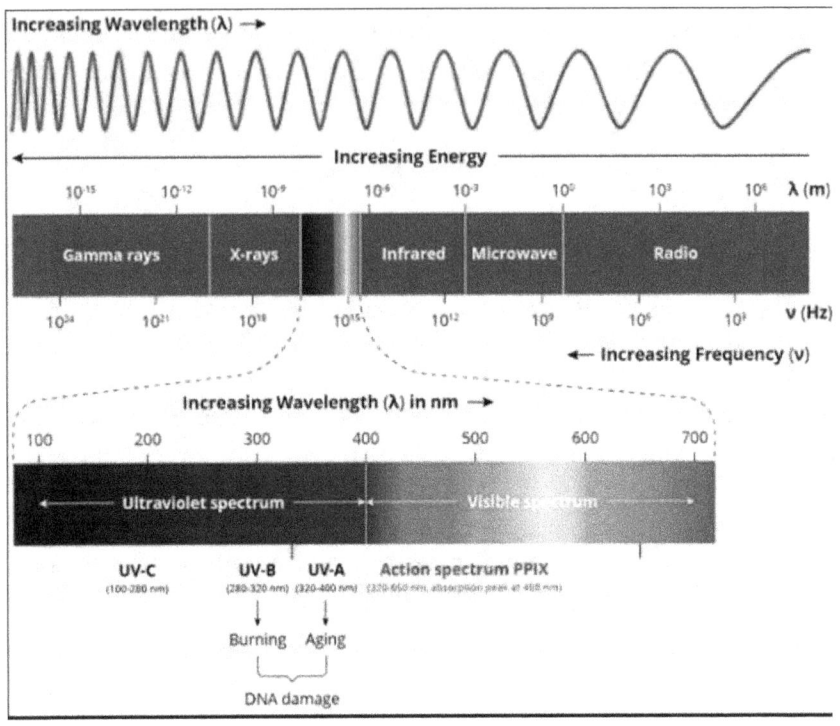

We only see a tiny fraction of that spectrum. When we are in pitch-black darkness, light is still present, but we humans do not see it. X-Rays for example penetrate straight through you, making little holes through your body. Your body must repair the damage every day, and after 60 years or so, it starts to become obvious you cannot repair the damage fast enough.

Is that how God is present everywhere? When God is talking with Job, one of the questions is, 'Where is the way where light dwelleth?' Nobody knows what light is. We can all see what it does, and its effect, but we do not know what it is! If the spirit of God is light itself, it makes sense that He is present everywhere as light is indeed everywhere in some form or another. Even radio waves are a form of light.

In Psalm 139:12:

12 "Yea, the darkness hideth not from thee; **but the night shineth as the day**: the darkness and the light are both alike to thee."

If we could see all parts of the spectrum, even the night would be well lit. Look through some good quality night vision goggles to get a feel for it.

The speed of light is something that has been measured for over 150 years and has been agreed that the speed of light is decreasing. In 1956 the atomic clock was invented. This clock was then used to measure the speed of light. The atomic clock is based on the wavelength of a $Cesium_{133}$ atom. The clock itself is based on the speed of light. If there is a clock, based on the speed of light and we measure the speed of light with it, then how will you catch the speed of light if it were to change? The speed of light is not a constant and can be affected by gravity such as black holes. It has been demonstrated in multiple lab tests that the speed of light can be both accelerated and slowed down. In January 2001, two groups of US scientists had slowed down light to a dead stop. Visible light at least, can be slowed by passing through denser matter such as water.

The redshift is something known in astronomy. When the light goes through a prism, we can see the light gets broken up into the colours of the rainbow. When starlight is analysed, it is done in a similar manner as elements burn different colours. So, by looking at the starlight you can work out what elements are burning. Most of these however lean more over to the red side of the spectrum. Hence the term redshift. In school, most are taught that this is caused by something known as the Doppler Effect. The Doppler Effect causes a sound to be higher as a train or plane approaches and lower as it passes. This happens because the sound waves are 'squashed' as they move forward to the observer. As something moves away the light waves are wider which fits under the red side of the spectrum. If they were to be moving closer, they would fall under the blue shift of the spectrum.

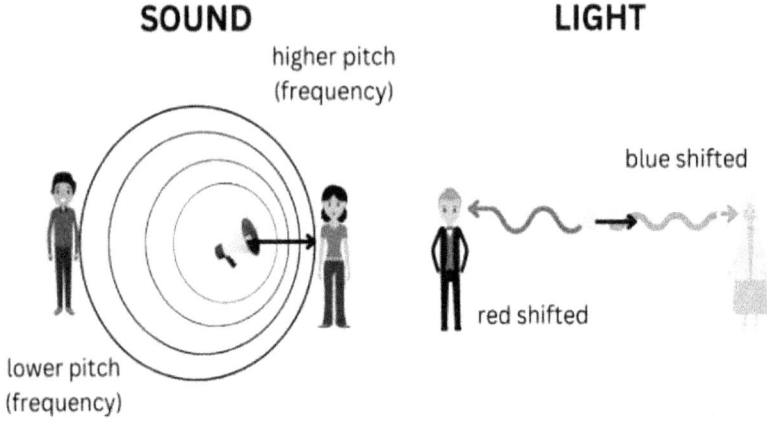

Image taken from sciencenotes.org

At least that is the theory behind it and that is what is taught. This theory is at least reasonable, but it does not tell you how far away something is. This cannot be proven by any reasonable doubt. Interesting to note though is that there are 17 times in the Bible where it mentions that God stretched out the heavens. It's mentioned in Isaiah 42:5, and again in Isaiah 45:12:

¹² "I have made the earth, and created man upon it: I, even my hands, **have stretched out the heavens**, and all their host have I commanded." (Isaiah 45:12)

Then again in Jeremiah 10:12:

¹² "He hath made the earth by his power, he hath established the world by his wisdom, **and hath stretched out the heavens by his discretion.**"

This stretching is also mentioned in Psalm 104:2, Isaiah 44:22, 51:13, and Zechariah 12:1. You can do a fun test just by drawing dots on a balloon and then blowing it up and watching it as it stretches. Blow it up one puff at a time and see how much it moves.

I wouldn't argue that the stars are moving away. The evolutionist will argue that they all used to be together, as this forms the basis of their Big Bang Theory. The Bible teaches that God made the Earth first, and made the stars also, then stretched out the heavens. We know that a prism breaks up the light as the different colours are different wavelengths. Maybe the redshift is caused by the fact the light is moving through space and thus being bent and affected by all the things in its path before reaching our eyes. Such as black holes and other stars. Gravity is a weak force but is far-reaching. Black holes are known to be what they are because even the light is affected by them.

In summary, the speed of light is not a constant, it is affected by gravity and can be slowed down and sped up in a laboratory. It was faster in the past. God made them closer originally then stretched them out for reasons unknown, but the simple reality is that the expansion of the universe discovered by observation, was noted in the Bible centuries ago. It's about time science caught up!

Role of Women in the Church

This topic is sure to light a fire under some people! But what does the scripture say regarding women taking leadership roles in the church?

1 Timothy 2:11-12:

"Let the woman learn in silence with all subjection.

But I suffer not a woman to teach, nor to usurp authority over the man, but to be in silence."

1 Corinthians 14:34-35:

34 Let your women keep silence in the churches: for it is not permitted unto them to speak; but they are commanded to be under obedience as also saith the law.

35 And if they will learn anything, let them ask their husbands at home: for it is a shame for women to speak in the church."

I can sense the discomfort already! But what about Deborah in the book of Judges! See there is a great female leader, anointed by God. I wouldn't argue she was one of the great leaders. Back then it would have been the synagogue rather than a church, the priest being the equivalent to a Senior Pastor. Deborah was an anointed woman but God did not make her a priest, however. She could lead worship and the military but not the church. God didn't make any women priests. All the priests were to be men and descendants of Aran. It only mentions about speaking in the church. The only ruler of Israel who was a woman was the daughter of Jezebel, Althaliah, who then ordered the massacre of the royal family. She was demon led.

Speaking of Jezebel, during her time there were three spirits at work. Jezebel was the wife of the King at the time, Ahab. Jezebel was seductive, domineering, and highly controlling, while Ahab was passive, indifferent, and silent. These traits which many women do not find attractive and do not want in their men ironically. Both of these two spirits were fighting against the Godly spirit of the prophet Elijah. These three spirits are still around today but working through different people, places, and times. People today have just accepted the Jezebel spirit in their churches. Something which Jesus gives a warning about in Revelation 2:20-21:

"Notwithstanding I have a few things against thee, because thou sufferest that woman Jezebel, which calleth herself a prophetess, to teach and to seduce my servants to commit fornication, and to eat things sacrificed unto idols.

And I gave her space to repent of her fornication; and she repented not."

The word 'sufferest' used here is the word for tolerance today. People have placed tolerance in the place of repentance. Jesus is warning us not to tolerate that woman 'Jezebel', she will cause my people to fornicate. Something God's people have been judged for time and time again and still don't seem to get it. The fact that He uses the name Jezebel could even suggest that is the name of the spirit, as when Jesus mentions her by name, over 1000 years later because it is the same spirit. She also had time to repent and chose not to. Elijah pushed back against Jezebel, while Ahab tolerated her.

In today's times though, Jesus will be the one pushing back against Jezebel and the churches tolerating it. If you do challenge this kind of mentality what will happen is they will go online, find many others filled with the Jezebel spirit, and then paint the picture of oppression in the church crying they are intolerant. But stand firm and keep the spirit of Elijah! For even Jesus will not tolerate Jezebel! Do not be like Ahab, sometimes we need to just do what needs to be done. I'd like to point out that both men and women can possess all three spirits. The Jezebel spirit is not just in women, the same is true for the Ahab and Elijah spirits. The spirit of Jezebel likes being in control so getting rid of it is a lot more difficult. Jezebel is all about control as opposed to submitting yourself willingly to God's will. The Jezebel spirit is all about control and will use the scriptures to use and deceive others. Satan did the same thing, which is why you need to know the scriptures for yourself. If they cannot teach, they will push their agenda on social media and seduce the Lord's servants. If you tolerate Jezebel in any area, they will take more and more. You can spot the Jezebel spirit by observing what they hate.

Authority. The Jezebel spirit hates being under any kind of authority and will seek control and want to be fiercely independent.

Telling them no. The personality changes as they are used to getting what they want. They will attempt to threaten you and say all manner of evil against you falsely. The same thing happened when Potiphar's wife tried to seduce Joseph, but Joseph was loyal to God which resulted in him being falsely accused and imprisoned. (Genesis 39)

They do not like losing. The prophet Elijah had a bounty placed on his head when he commanded fire to rain from the heavens (1 Kings 18), thus taking out the false prophets of Jezebel.

They do not like rebukes and correction. Whenever they are confronted, they will disagree. They dismiss what God says in favour of their agenda. There is no repentance.

Man-hating. Jezebel does not like or respect any men she encounters. Killing many of them in the scriptures to get what she wants. Maybe caused by a bad relationship and it changed them. These people need help, these bad relationships have changed them but not for the better. Jezebel hates Elijah because he is the godliest, she makes it her personal mission to destroy him and considers him the greatest threat.

Being truthful. Jezebel is consistently dishonest as it is about control. This sounds a lot like our politicians! They say and do anything to get their way. They will get their story out first to control the narrative and silence the full picture. You'll see this in the media frequently.

They do not like being preached at and want to remain under the radar. Jezebel killed all the preachers except Elijah.

We must resist the Jezebel spirit in both our churches and in our personal lives. Jesus will rebuke it if we do not.

Historical and traditional interpretations of these and other passages have led to the view that church leadership roles, particularly those of Pastor or Elder, are reserved for men. The theological view holds that men and women have complementary but distinct roles. In this framework, men are seen as having leadership roles in both the family and the church. Both sexes are equal in God's eyes, but each sex is better suited to specific roles, and have specific duties. Men for example cannot carry children. We'd be extinct if they did, that's why God left that to women.

It is also important to note that the greatest testimony in history, the risen Lord, was given to Mary Magdalene. It was also another Mary who carried Jesus Christ. The two most important events in our history were the responsibility of women. I'd also like to point out that when the soldiers came to get Jesus, the 12 disciples ran for it, but the women stayed. It was shameful for the men to run for it! It is society and Satan who are trying to attack the family unit and God's ordained order which is causing rebellion. This male leadership is also part of the curse, and it is a curse for both sexes, as mentioned in Genesis 3:16.

16 "Unto the woman he said, I will greatly multiply thy sorrow and thy conception; in sorrow thou shalt bring forth children; and thy desire shall be to thy husband, and he shall rule over thee."

God's order has not changed, and neither has the curse. Eve was the one who first ate the fruit and thus sinned first. But the scriptures say, by one MAN death entered into the world, and death by sin. This is because Adam also ate, and he was the head of the family so the buck ultimately stops with him. The woman is to submit to male leadership and male leadership is to submit to Christ because he is head of the church. It's also very interesting that every woman I have ever spoken to about their ideal partner, 99% of them talk about having a man to take the lead in the relationship, this is because a house divided against itself cannot stand as mentioned in Matthew 12:25 and Mark 3:25. The Lord has appointed one as the lead like Jesus is head of the church. Nobody is above the Lord.

Men also feel a strong desire to provide and lead the family. It's almost like it has been hardwired into us by our creator! It is also interesting, and kind of ironic, that one of the most-sold books for women in recent years (50 Shades of Grey) is all about a man dominating a woman! Of course, there is a healthy and unhealthy way to do that. But Genesis 3:16, is saying that a woman's desire shall be to her husband. A component of the breakdown of society is because we are rebelling against this order. This should not be a surprise. Society is rejecting God's Word, and then wondering why everything around us is collapsing!

If the military is preparing for a conflict and there is a private and the sergeant. It is the sergeant's job to give the orders and the private's job to execute said orders. The orders flow in only one direction and do not work in reverse.

Now you can hear the objections, "What about Galatians 3:28?"

[28] "There is neither Jew nor Greek, there is neither bond nor free, there is neither male nor female: for ye are all one in Christ Jesus."

See, this says we are all one in Christ Jesus! We are indeed. However, there is a defined structure in place. We are one **in** Christ, we are not above Christ though. Some scholars argue that the prohibitions against women speaking or leading in church in the New Testament were specific to the cultural and social contexts of the time, rather than universal, timeless commands. Others argue the Holy Spirit distributes spiritual gifts, including leadership and teaching, to both men and women without distinction. I would lovingly disagree, Jesus said until heaven and earth pass and not one yot or tittle shall pass from the law until ALL be fulfilled. It is not yet all fulfilled. If so, that would mean God's Word has changed. It hasn't, no scripture is open to any private interpretation.

In Malachi 3:6 the Lord declares He changes not. The scripture will interpret itself, just read it. The mention of the role of women in the church appears in the New Testament. This does not mean men and women cannot get a prophetic word. My wife and I will often discuss such topics when she has been given some form of revelation. But how it gets delivered though is important. Most of God's messages were delivered through the anointed prophets. God made it clear that you will know a prophet if what they say comes to pass as it was given to them. In our military example above, the sergeant is often relying on orders from above, to be flowed down through the proper channels. The question I have for you, is do you trust God's order? Even if we do not understand His reasoning?

What About Other Religions?

There have been thousands of so-called 'gods' in man's history. The scoffers will no doubt point that out, why should I follow yours? It is straightforward to disprove those false gods with a bit of study, this topic could be an entire book on its own and one I would encourage you to study. You must know why you follow Jesus for yourself. The two biggest religions in the world are Christianity and Islam so for the purposes of this book I will focus on Islam and why I do not follow Islam.

Before we continue, I would like to point out that many Muslims I have met are just like everyone else. I do however think they have been deceived into following something false. The Muslims I have met do not study the Quran for themselves and are instead taught it by the Imams. Much like the churches, they leave out the parts that would make many uncomfortable. Many of them have grown up in and around the mosques, much like some of the Christians I meet, because they have grown up with it, few question it and ask if what they are following is right.

It is exceptionally hard for a Muslim to convert; most are from honour backgrounds where you can disgrace not only your living family but the legacy of their grandparents also. You can still be killed for leaving the Islamic faith, known as the law of apostasy and if you are wrong, the Quarn says you are going to hell for believing Jesus is God! Many Muslims who come from overseas see places like the UK and USA that claim to be Christian nations, and when they see all the immorality in society, they impute all of that on Christian values! When we haven't acted like a Christian nation for some time.

Islam is the second-largest religion currently and is growing. When I started on my journey, I looked at Islam, because I wanted to know what was true. This topic could be an entire book on its own, but for this book, I'm just going to focus on why I rejected Islam as being true.

Muhammad is considered a prophet but didn't prophesy anything. There are no prophecies in the Quran. There are many in the Bible which have come to pass. Such as the Messiah coming in on a donkey and being rejected by His own people.

Islam accepts Jesus was virgin born, many believing He was the only sinless prophet and will return to initiate the last days. This then makes no sense as to why they would then follow Muhammad over Jesus. They don't accept Jesus as God, and state that if you do believe that, you will be going to hell, as mentioned in the Quran chapter 4:71 as well as 5:72. In John 1:1 it says; "In the beginning was the word and the word was with God and the word was God." Verse 14 says, "..and the Word was made flesh, and dwelt among us." They do not believe He claimed to be God, which He does, as mentioned in the earlier chapter. In John, it is claimed the word became flesh and dwelt with us.

In Sura 4:80 – 'He who obeys the messenger has obeyed Allah.' - This is Muhammad himself saying this, the speaker is the messenger, commanding the same obedience given only to Allah. Jesus says the most important commandment is to love the Lord with all your heart, mind, and soul and the second is much like it, not the messenger.

There is no assurance of their salvation. Many Muslims believe in good works, but ultimately it is at the discretion of Allah as to whether you go to heaven or not. Muhammad himself did not know if he was going to heaven.

Verses such as Surah 18:86: 'Until, when he reached the setting of the sun, he found it set in a spring of murky water...' – The sun does not set in water, and there are many other errors besides this one.

There are 109 commands in the Quran to kill all non-Muslims, Surah 4:89 as an example. The Bible says as one of the Ten Commandments, "You shall not commit murder." The God of the Bible wants all to come to repentance and wants **no one** to perish, regardless of background.

In Islam, God requires you to send your son to die for him. Christianity, God sends His son to die for you and take the payment for your sins.

Islam seeks to eliminate all the Jews. In the Bible, the Jews are God's people. Not because He cares about them more, but because they are meant to be a peculiar people. Strange that in Israel, where there are many nations surrounding it, when you look at Google Maps, Israel is green on the map, while the surrounding nations are not. Incidentally, killing all the Jews is exactly what Satan wants. God is to provide the Messiah through them, so by eliminating them that cannot happen.

Islam comes from Ishmael, the son of Hagar. God requires a man and a woman to be married. Ishmael was illegitimate.

Various passages to fight and make war against unbelievers such as 9:73 / 8:39 / 9:5 and 9:29.

The Quran doesn't accept Jesus died on the cross. In Surah 157, He was neither killed, nor was He crucified but so it appeared to them. It denies the death of Christ on the cross. It suggests that someone other than Jesus was crucified in His place. This is despite evidence outside of the Bible that He was. That alone challenges the Qurans' reliability. The reason you believe He died on the cross is because Allah tricked everyone, I know of one master deceiver and that is Satan. I would also argue that Satan does not want you to put your hope and faith in Jesus.

Muslims often claim the Bible has been corrupted. There are many verses in the Quran, that if the Bible had been corrupted, then Allah doesn't know that. In Surah 5:47: 'And let the People of the Gospel judge by what Allah has revealed therein. And whoever does not judge by what Allah has revealed – then it is those who are the defiantly disobedient.' - In other words, Christians are to judge by the Gospel, not by the Quran, and we are rebels if we don't. The Quran assumes the Gospel still has reliable scriptures. It commands us to judge by the Gospel and then denies Jesus on the cross... If we follow the Quran, we have to reject the Quran.

They claim the Bible has been corrupted but there are 12 verses in the Quran which mention the Gospel. Surah 3:3, Surah 3:48, Surah 3:65, Surah 5:46-47, Surah 5:66, Surah 5:68, Surah 5:110, Surah 7:157, Surah 9:111, Surah 48:29 and Surah 57:27. Some of these are clear while others require context. I would encourage you to read these and the surrounding passages for yourself. In Surah 3:2-4 it states that God sent down the book upon thee in truth, **confirming what was before it, and He sent down the Torah and the Gospel aforetime, as a guidance to mankind.** If Muslims claim the gospel was corrupted (usually by Paul) they are admitting Allah failed. It effectively confirms the Gospel. I would urge both Christians and Muslims to study this for themselves and not to confuse faith with ignorance.

The Quran always criticises Christians for not obeying what was revealed in the Gospel, not once does it condemn our scriptures or hint that the Gospel cannot be trusted.

Christians and non-believers of the Quran are horribly mistreated throughout the world. Once the community is strong enough Allah commands to fight against those who do not believe in Allah in Surah 9:29. It is a command to fight those who do not believe in Allah, nor acknowledge the Religion of Truth, from among The People of The Book until they pay the tax. Allah commands Christians and Jews to be fought until we pay the tax and acknowledge ourselves as inferior. The Bible teaches everyone is valuable in God's eyes, not just Christians, and calls for the repentance of all.

The evidence of Muhammad's life comes much later after his death than that of Jesus.

Muslims are taught Muhammad was an amazing man, a great diplomat, general, husband, and leader. Muslims praise the Muhammad they have been taught by the Imams. Dig deeper though and the historical evidence suggests otherwise. The historical Muhammad is very different to those in the heart of most Muslims. Most Muslims do believe it to be a religion of peace, with the jihad being 'cancelled' by peace. Groups like Hamas, ISIS, etcetera, follow the actual teachings of Muhammad.

After a lot of digging, prayer, and soul searching, I concluded Islam is false, I personally believe it is Satan's counterfeit religion to deceive many. If you are a Muslim reading this, I would encourage you to study both with a critical eye and look for the historical evidence and hadiths for yourself and bypass the Imams. Seek, and you will find. If you are a Christian, I would also encourage you to seek out what the Muslims believe, if you know any, invite them to dinner! Relationships are built with time, love, and care. We are all made in God's image and God wants as many in Heaven as possible.

Conclusion

In every part of the Bible, we will 100% find something we disagree with or do not like. This is irrelevant though, what does God say? It isn't what the Bible says that is the issue. It is, do you believe what it says, and do you trust in Him and his ways? His ways are higher than ours. Anything else, is us rebelling and making a God in OUR liking and OUR image, doing what we think is right, as the book of Judges says. We will happily accept His salvation and His grace, but not so much His leadership. God is the lawgiver, and we need to leave the worldly teachings and come over to God's and lean not on our own understanding. Jesus himself does NOT tolerate some things.

In the Old Testament in the book of Judges, among others, God tells the people of Israel not to tolerate some things. When you go into the land you shall make no covenant with the inhabitants, and you are to destroy their altars (Judges 2:1-3). They were not to tolerate false Gods and religions and not to even marry those who would lead them astray. Multiple times they do not OBEY His voice and do not heed the warnings and as a result, these false gods (demons) become a snare to them. People say they don't like the God of the Old Testament as He declares war. So does Jesus, in Revelation, He comes to start a war to end them all and put an end to all evil. He also states in Revelation:

[20] "Notwithstanding I have a few things against thee, because thou sufferest that woman Jezebel, which calleth herself a prophetess, to teach and to seduce my servants to commit fornication, and to eat things sacrificed unto idols." (Revelation 2:20)

The spirit of Jezebel, who was around during the times of Elijah, is still present now. Tolerance is the opposite of what repentance is and leads to false teaching and sexual immorality. If we tolerate that woman, Jezebel, she will teach you it is okay to fornicate. It is not. If we allow evil, evil will flourish.

Which is what we are seeing in society today. People who think people are good, all have locks on their doors, don't they? Put your trust and hope in our Lord. When we find something in the Bible we do not like or agree with, the fault is ours, we are the ones who are wrong. God does not repent to us for upsetting us, it is the other way around. We do not see the end from the beginning, He does. We must trust that He knows what He is doing to deliver us. Diamonds are formed under great pressure. For us to be our best, we too must come under pressure to come out refined.

Christianity is the only belief system where your works have nothing to do with getting into heaven or not. The others are based on good works, and whether you realise it or not, that belief is trying to blackmail God for entry into heaven. I don't think that will go well come judgement day. Society is doing what is right, in their own eyes. They did the same thing multiple times in the Bible. In the book of Judges 2:7-12 they did evil in the sight of the Lord and provoked Him to anger. God gets angry. If you are not getting angry as a Christian, you are devoid of the spirit. Anger is a form of showing love. In the story, the people following Joshua did not know the Lord. They were not taught about Him and His ways. Have you noticed society has been removing God from their classrooms, then wondering why everything has become so wicked... If you DO NOT raise your children in the ways of the Lord, someone else will and it WILL NOT be good. God will only bless His divine design. Eventually, God will have to intervene in this wicked and perverted society.

Romans 2:4:

4 "Or despisest thou the riches of his goodness and forbearance and longsuffering; not knowing that the goodness of God leadeth thee to repentance?"

The reason God is patient with us, is so we can come to repentance. It is not because He is tolerating our evil.

2 Peter 3:9

9 "The Lord is not slack concerning his promise, as some men count slackness; but is longsuffering to us-ward, not willing that any should perish, **but that all should come to repentance."**

Chapter 5
The End Times

The end times are something I hear very little about in modern churches. They seem too scared to even touch on the subject! The rapture of the church and God's wrath falling on mankind seem taboo topics today. You'll occasionally hear some people say, 'I've heard end times preached on for 50 years and it hasn't happened yet!' I'm sure there have been many times throughout history when it seemed like the end, and events such as World War II come to mind. I believe we are now in a time in which the Bible says more about it than when Jesus walked the shores. To know if that statement is true, **you must know the scriptures for yourself**. The end times are mentioned throughout the Bible, most notably in Daniel, Ezekiel, Joel, Isaiah, the Gospels, Thessalonians and of course, Revelation.

For Christians, understanding the end times prophecies is essential as we are required to be able to understand the signs of the times. The religious leaders of Jesus' time missed the signs of His coming, how much more important is it then than we recognise the times we find ourselves in? The disciples asked Jesus directly and He answered them, which can be found in Matthew 24, Mark 13, and Luke 21. One of the biggest signs will be the sun and the moon going dark and a great and terrible earthquake.

The end times are known in many cultures. They are referenced not only in the Bible but the Quran, and stories in our history such as Norse mythology. Many Christians I speak to today believe we have now entered into that time, and it is easy to see why. Violence against others is on the rise, and so is sexual immorality, more frequent disasters such as earthquakes have increased in both frequency and intensity, with more intense weather, and knowledge has increased just as the Bible has predicted. There have always been wars and rumours of wars, but this is the first time that all these signs are now happening at once.

The biggest tell-tale sign is the acceptance of things the Bible clearly condemns. If you tolerate it, evil will dominate, and it will not stop itself. The wickedness of man is on full display, with everyone doing what is right in their own eyes. Not what is right in the Lord's eyes, which is often the opposite. The Lord has told us in advance what we can expect though, by looking at the current state of the world and comparing it to the Word, then you should not fear, you know the plan already!

The teachings on the end times in the Bible carry profound implications for believers, shaping their faith, conduct, and outlook on the future. Believers are called to live in a state of readiness, knowing that Christ could return at any moment. This readiness involves maintaining a strong relationship with God and living a life that reflects His values. We are made in His image after all! Jesus repeatedly stressed the need for vigilance and to watch therefore and pray always that you may be accounted worthy to escape all these things that shall come to pass and stand before the Son of Man (Matthew 24:42 and Luke 21:36). Prayer is exceptionally important if we are to live a Holy life. Prayer is speaking to God directly; genuine prayer will help us avoid sin and grow in righteousness.

The prophecies of the end times provide hope and encouragement to believers, assuming that despite current difficulties, God's victory is certain. We need to understand that present sufferings will be temporary, and that eternal glory awaits those believers who endure trials and take comfort in knowing that Christ will come to establish

His kingdom and provide solace, wiping away all tears, no more death and sorrow, for the former things have passed away (Revelation 21:4).

The knowledge of the end times should motivate believers to share the gospel with urgency, knowing that time for repentance is limited! Jesus' command for us to make disciples of all nations takes on a greater urgency in the end times. We are called to spread the gospel so that more people can be saved before Christ's return. It is why recognising the signs of the times is so important!

50 years ago, would have been the 1970s, at the point of writing. How much has changed since then? The biggest three that come to mind are the internet, mobile phones, particularly smartphones, and computers. In the 1970s we had to store many documents in filling cabinets and spent however long shifting through them! With the use of computers, we can now file and retrieve documents in seconds. With the internet, something that happened mere moments ago can be seen on your phone! Not possible 50 years ago. The rise of the internet has also led to an increase in both knowledge and deception. In Daniel 12:4:

4 "But thou, O Daniel, shut up the words, and seal the book, even to the time of the end: many shall run to and fro, and **knowledge shall be increased.**"

This says to shut up the book, it's not for you Daniel, it's for people coming after you. I'm sure Daniel didn't understand, but knowledge today is widely available. Unfortunately, that knowledge has not led to increased wisdom, because the fear of the Lord, is the beginning of wisdom and people do not fear the Lord anymore and have gravely mistaken His patience for tolerance and inaction. He was patient with the people of Noah's time, but eventually that patience wore out, and the floods came.

1 Timothy 4:1

¹ "Now the Spirit speaketh expressly, that in the latter times some shall depart from the faith, giving heed to seducing spirits, and doctrines of devils"

So many are now lost in the temptations of the world but you can test to see if the spirits are from God or not.

1 John 4:1

¹ "Beloved, believe not every spirit, but try the spirits whether they are of God: because many false prophets are gone out into the world."

There are many 'wolves in sheep's clothing' around today trying to convince Christians that certain behaviours are okay and as a result, are leading them astray. They are not okay, and God's Word clearly says differently. The test is to compare what is being taught against what is written and taught in the Bible. Many churches, along with many other nations, have now accepted same-sex marriage and that is clearly against the teaching of scripture. They are no longer on Team Jesus but have become apostates for Team Satan. We are required to test what is being said:

¹⁰ "And the brethren immediately sent away Paul and Silas by night unto Berea: who coming thither went into the synagogue of the Jews.

¹¹ These were more noble than those in Thessalonica, **in that they received the word with all readiness of mind, and searched the scriptures daily, whether those things were so.**" (Acts 17:10-11)

The Jews listened to Paul and Silas and then went and checked the scriptures, they were considered noble for doing so. Do not just accept every teaching. Including what you have read in this book! Go and examine the scriptures for yourself and ask God to illuminate what you are reading. The Holy Spirit promised to teach you **all** things. Take Him up on that promise. Diligently study the scriptures while asking the Holy Spirit directly to teach it to you. You do not need a degree in theology, only those who financially rely upon that will tell you that you do. You just need your Bible, and time in prayer.

John 14:26

26 "But the Comforter, which is the Holy Ghost, whom the Father will send in my name, **he shall teach you all things,** and bring all things to your remembrance, whatsoever I have said unto you."

By doing this you present yourself approved to God as we read earlier in 2 Timothy 2:15:

15 "**Study to shew thyself approved unto God**, a workman that needeth not to be ashamed, rightly dividing the word of truth."

In Timothy 3:16-17:

"All scripture is given by inspiration of God, and is profitable for doctrine, for reproof, for correction, for instruction in righteousness:

That the man of God may be perfect, thoroughly furnished unto all good works."

These false teachers will twist God's Word, just as Satan first did to Eve, from changing God hath said to, hath God said. Christians today have not used the scriptures for reproof, correction or instruction in righteousness in recent times and it shows by the breakdown of society. The evil we see in our world today is partly our fault, the result is evil has flourished, and as mentioned in Romans 1:24-28:

24 "Wherefore **God also gave them up to uncleanness through the lusts of their own hearts**, to dishonour their own bodies between themselves:

25 **Who changed the truth of God into a lie, and worshipped and served the creature more than the Creator**, who is blessed for ever. Amen.

26 **For this cause God gave them up unto vile affections: for even their women did change the natural use into that which is against nature:**

27 **And likewise also the men, leaving the natural use of the woman, burned in their lust one toward another; men with men working that which is unseemly, and receiving in themselves that recompence of their error which was meet.**

28 And even as **they did not like to retain God in their knowledge, God gave them over to a reprobate mind, to do those things which are not convenient;**"

The people of today do not want to retain God in their knowledge, do they? It is all unfolding, just as the Bible predicts. It was a similar story in the book of Judges when the people did not seek God for guidance.

2 Peter 3:16:

16 "As also in all his epistles, speaking in them of these things; in which are some things hard to be understood, which they that are unlearned and unstable wrest, as they do also the other scriptures, unto their own destruction."

This twisted teaching has led many to find teachers who want to have their ears tickled and told what they want to hear and not what they need to hear, teaching there are many ways to heaven when the Bible clearly teaches that Jesus is the only way. 2 Timothy 4:3-4:

"For the time will come when they will not endure sound doctrine; but after their own lusts shall they heap to themselves teachers, having itching ears;

And they shall turn away their ears from the truth, and shall be turned unto fables."

It is important you know the scriptures for yourself to avoid being led astray. I write this as a matter of urgency. If we have indeed entered into the end times, which I now believe we have, every single day that passes is a day closer to the return of Jesus. You must be steadfast in the faith and pray always that you are counted worthy to escape all the judgements incoming. The door is narrow, make EVERY EFFORT to get through the door before the host comes to close that door.

Deception will be rife in the end times, and it is rife today. The rise of the internet has made it so. Anyone can put anything on the internet, and some will just believe it without doing any research, they deceive themselves. Do you know of anyone who has had their identity stolen or fallen for an online scam?

Some churches are prime examples of deception, they accept things that are clearly against scripture. Many churches have also deviated considerably from what the scriptures actually say and injected some of their worldly lusts and desires into their doctrine. They have moved the barrier so far out that what they preach does not match the scriptures. Many are now Christian in name only, and as a result, are being led astray. Turn away from teachers who stray from what

God's Word says. But this should not be a surprise to those who read their Bibles for themselves and do not rely on others to teach it to them. These are what Jesus calls the lukewarm crowd.

We cannot afford to be lukewarm Christians. God sets the standard, not us. If we disagree, it is us who are wrong. We can continue in our rebellion, or we can repent and follow the Lord's leadership. One thing to note though, staying in rebellion is unwise, you can argue with the Lord if you want, but He is undefeated. That does not mean to be unloving, uncaring, etcetera, but we must not endorse sinful behaviour. We are meant to call it out when we see it. Jesus declares in Matthew 18:15-17:

15 "Moreover if thy brother shall trespass against thee, go and tell him his fault between thee and him alone: if he shall hear thee, thou hast gained thy brother.

16 But if he will not hear thee, then take with thee one or two more, that in the mouth of two or three witnesses every word may be established.

17 And if he shall neglect to hear them, tell it unto the church: but if he neglect to hear the church, let him be unto thee as an heathen man and a publican"

Many are not doing what they do in line with the scriptures. When so-called religious leaders bless things like gay marriage or idolatry or bowing to false prophets and images, run in the opposite direction. No pastor or leader has any right to bless something God himself would not and they are leading you astray. You are better off reading and studying the Bible for yourself than you are attending a church preaching the world's message. Some in the church are not saved and will betray you given the chance. These people will have a shock when the Lord comes to rapture His people. I do not say such things to deliberately antagonise, cause mistrust or otherwise, you know it is the truth and the truth often upsets people. They'd rather be told comforting lies that make them feel good. Trust God for your salvation only. Not me, your pastor, your spouse, or yourself, but God only.

Feelings incidentally are something that you need to be really careful about. They make up an important part of your intelligence but are very easy to be deceived by. Remember the story of Jacob and Esau. Their father Isaac had lost his sight and gave Esau's blessing to Jacob because he went by what he felt over the word being spoken. You sound like Jacob but feel like Esau.

Genesis 27:20-21:

[20] "And Isaac said unto his son, How is it that thou hast found it so quickly, my son? And he said, Because the LORD thy God brought it to me.

[21] And Isaac said unto Jacob, Come near, I pray thee, that I may feel thee, my son, whether thou be my very son Esau or not."

When you make decisions based solely on your feelings, you will be deceived. This is exactly what we are witnessing in the world today. So many people, Christian and non-Christian alike are prioritising their feelings over factual information and what they can see. Some feelings are out of bounds.

1 John 2:15-17:

15 "Love not the world, neither the things that are in the world. If any man love the world, the love of the Father is not in him.

16 For all that is in the world, the lust of the flesh, and the lust of the eyes, and the pride of life, is not of the Father, but is of the world.

17 And the world passeth away, and the lust thereof: but he that doeth the will of God abideth for ever."

Remember God kept Adam and Eve from knowing evil. Keeping that knowledge withheld was for their benefit. Just because something looks and feels good to you, doesn't mean it is good for you. Everything sinful, satanic and negative for you always comes disguised as something captivating and fun. Producing pleasure at first before slowly producing pain and regrets. The people who tell you **not to engage in your lusts** are those who truly love you. You will hear the world say that love is love. Love conquers all etcetera. But that is only a partial truth. People will say, how can you, as a

Christian be against love? But loving someone means telling them the truth, real love is wanting and acting in the best interest of the other person. People today are confusing love with lust. Loving, the wrong person, or object or coming from the wrong source can be sinful and lead you straight to destruction.

Romans 1: 17-29:

17 "For therein is the righteousness of God revealed from faith to faith: as it is written, **The just shall live by faith.**

18 For the wrath of God is revealed from heaven against all ungodliness and unrighteousness of men, who hold the truth in unrighteousness;

19 Because that which may be known of God is manifest in them; for God hath shewed it unto them. 20 For the invisible things of him from the creation of the world are clearly seen, being understood by the things that are made, even his eternal power and Godhead; so that they are without excuse:

Because that, when they knew God, they glorified him not as God, neither were thankful; but became vain in their imaginations, and their foolish heart was darkened.

Professing themselves to be wise, they became fools,

23 And changed the glory of the uncorruptible God into an image made like to corruptible man, and to birds, and fourfooted beasts, and creeping things.

24 Wherefore God also gave them up to uncleanness through the lusts of their own hearts, to dishonour their own bodies between themselves:

25 **"Who changed the truth of God into a lie, and worshipped and served the creature more than the Creator**, who is blessed for ever. Amen.

26**For this cause God gave them up unto vile affections: for even their women did change the natural use into that which is against nature:**

27 **And likewise also the men, leaving the natural use of the woman, burned in their lust one toward another; men with men**

working that which is unseemly, and receiving in themselves that recompence of their error which was meet.

28 And even as they did not like to retain God in their knowledge, **God gave them over to a reprobate mind, to do those things which are not convenient;**

29 Being filled with all unrighteousness, fornication, wickedness, covetousness, maliciousness; full of envy, murder, debate, deceit, malignity; whisperers,"

Nobody I meet thinks it is okay to be sexually attracted to a minor. Incidentally, the Israelites made a golden calf and worshipped that. They loved their image over the creator, and they were punished for it. If we are in Christ we are no longer of this world and our actions should reflect that. If they do not, we cannot call ourselves born again. I love my children, I do NOT give them what they want when they want it, just because they want it. Some of the things they want will put them on a path of destruction and I love them enough to stand in the way. It is precisely the reason Jesus took the punishment for our sins because He doesn't want us to head into destruction either.

You will hear sermons that preach how much God wants to bless you. But how many sermons do you hear about sin, its consequences, and the fact you are one of the sinners? Many pastors today preach what people want to hear. Just as the Bible predicted in 2 Timothy 4:3-4:

3 "For the time will come when they will not endure sound doctrine; but after their own lusts shall they heap to themselves teachers, having itching ears;

⁴And they shall turn away their ears from the truth, and shall be turned unto fables."

We are to teach what the Bible actually says, not what we want it to say. If we are truly in Christ, the world will hate us for it. We are to follow God's Word NOT the world or its teachings. People suppress the Gospel message because it acts as a mirror to show us, that we are guilty of breaking God's laws. Come as you are, but don't stay as you are. Nobody wants to know that all their thoughts and actions will be judged someday. But here's the good news, God can transform you from the inside out and there is still time to ask!

When Jesus says many shall come in my name, how can we tell when the real Jesus will show up? The answer is found in Acts 1:9-11:

⁹ And when he had spoken these things, while they beheld, he was taken up; and a cloud received him out of their sight.

¹⁰ And while they looked stedfastly toward heaven as he went up, behold, two men stood by them in white apparel;

¹¹ Which also said, Ye men of Galilee, why stand ye gazing up into heaven? this same Jesus, which is taken up from you into heaven, shall so come in like manner as ye have seen him go into heaven."

Jesus was taken to Heaven in a cloud, and will return in a cloud. In today's world that is something you will see all around the globe at the same time. If He isn't in a cloud upon His return, then it is not Christ. Simple as that.

With just those examples a lot has changed in 50 years. The technology is available now to usher in the Anti-Christ and his regime. Where none may buy or sell without the 'Mark'.

The Mark of the Beast

There have been many theories behind what the mark will be. It has been believed that tattoos, barcodes, credit cards and microchips are the most common. I personally believe in the use of the microchip theory for several reasons. Time has a strange effect of making us complacent. If we had gone from trading goods and services to a mark in your hand, the people would have refused. We started trading with money, gold and silver, which went to paper money (backed by gold or something physical). Money is now a currency as opposed to being backed by something physical. From there it went to credit cards and numbers on screen. Now you can pay with your phone. How much longer before it is transferred to your hand? The technology is there today to do this. We have been microchipping pets for decades now. My belief is the mark will be a microchip of some capacity, and powered similarly to a pacemaker, but the world is slowly getting people to accept this mark, whatever it turns out to be. Satan isn't even trying to hide the plan anymore.

This image was taken in London in 2024.

The Bible warns that no one will be able to buy or sell without this mark, poor or rich, free or bond you will not be able to buy and sell. If that happened today, would you refuse? Many Christians I speak to say they won't take it. But will that be the case if they see their children starving because they cannot buy groceries? One thing the Bible makes clear though is that you will not be able to take this mark by accident. You will know what you are doing and will be declaring allegiance to the Anti-Christ.

One of the other things Jesus warms about in Matthew 24:10-14:
"And then shall many be offended, and shall betray one another.
And many false teachers shall rise, and shall deceive many.
And because iniquity shall abound, the love of many shall wax cold.
But he that shall endure unto the end, the same shall be saved.

And this gospel of the kingdom shall be preached in all the world for a witness unto all nations; and then shall the end come. "

Let's look at this. We touched on earlier about those who are offended. If you love God's law, you will not be offended as per Psalm 119:165. And iniquity shall abound. The word 'iniquity' means:

Complete injustice or wickedness.
Something unjust or wicked, sin.

How many hideous crimes do you hear about in today's world? Our moral decline can no longer be denied. It used to be that a murder would shock the entire nation, not much shocks us anymore. Violence has become so normalised through our media and what we consume. Whether that be movies, games, or music. This has not been an accident. The devil wants you to be desensitised to it, to think that your sins and behaviour are no big deal.

In the latter days, many shall betray one another. Otherwise known as apostasy. Judas was an apostate who also controlled the moneybox, which is why he got upset when the woman poured expensive oil on Jesus for His burial. Controlling the finances will highlight who the evil ones are, and who truly follow Christ. China currently has a social credit system. Limiting those who do not go along with the CCP's agenda. I hate to say it, but it is only a matter of time before something similar happens across the world, the people of God will then have to make a choice. Does the way you live your life make it obvious you follow Jesus? Those who are truly following the Lord will be hated and persecuted. Many in the church will go the way of the world and give up those who truly do follow Jesus. Nazi Germany gave up many Jews so they themselves would avoid persecution. When Christ's followers are targeted in the same manner you must stay the course.

One area we cannot ignore is found in Romans 13:1-2:

¹" Let every soul be subject unto the higher powers. For there is no power but of God: the powers that be are ordained of God.

² Whosoever therefore resisteth the power, resisteth the ordinance of God: and they that resist shall receive to themselves damnation."

We live in time when a lot of authority is against God and is the spirit of the Anti-Christ. This is pointing out authority is important to God, and there will be hierarchy. However, if the authority goes against God's Word, that is illegitimate authority. We are to submit to legitimate authority. If the authority is Godly, we are to submit to it. I cannot stress enough how important it is to REFUSE to take this mark. This will be choice that YOU may have to make. You will not be able to take this by accident. Since Covid, many places will not accept cash. If you only bring cash, you cannot go there. What I suspect will happen, is we will be slowly strangled out of society as opposed to a sudden acceptance of this mark.

Revelation 14:9-10:

⁹ "And the third angel followed them, saying with a loud voice, If **any man worship** the beast and his image, and receive his mark in his forehead, or in his hand,

¹⁰ The same shall drink of the wine of the wrath of God, which is poured out without mixture into the cup of his indignation; and he **shall be tormented with fire and brimstone in the presence of the holy angels, and in the presence of the Lamb**"

Those that do these things will feel the full force of the Lords anger.

Gods Wrath

God's wrath is a significant theme in the Bible, representing His righteous anger and judgement against sin, evil, and injustice. It is a complex concept that needs to be understood within the broader context of God's character, which includes His holiness, justice, love and mercy.

God's wrath is not arbitrary or capricious, but instead a righteous response to sin. Unlike human anger, which can be influenced by emotions and biases, God's wrath is always just, measured, and aligned with His perfect holiness and justice. God's wrath is often depicted as the necessary and rightful consequence of humanity's rebellion against His laws and commands. It serves as a demonstration of His commitment to uphold moral order and justice.

Many people today have taken advantage of God's patience. Claiming that He hasn't judged me yet, thus they continue in their sin. God's wrath however comes in two forms. The first comes in the form of passive wrath. The Bible talks about Jesus knocking on the door, and those who hear and open He will come and sup with them. He will not continue knocking, at that point comes stage one of judgement. He will give you up to indulge in your desires. This is a form of wrath because when we are left to our own devices, we often destroy ourselves, just look around at society, and it is evident God has abandoned them!

The second is what we know as divine judgement. The flood which was sent to cleanse the Earth of widespread wickedness. Sodom and Gomorrah, with these cities being destroyed with fire and brimstone because of grievous sins. This event illustrates God's intolerance of persistent sin and His willingness to execute judgement. The exile of Israel in 2 Kings 17 is noteworthy as the people of Israel and Judah experienced God's wrath through conquest and exile for repeatedly turning away from God, worshipping idols and engaging in sexual immorality and injustice.

Throughout the Old Testament, prophets like Isaiah, Jeremiah and Ezekiel warned of God's impending wrath if the people did not repent. These warnings often included calls to return to God, emphasizing His desire for repentance and restoration rather than destruction. Jesus spoke of God's wrath, particularly in terms of the final judgement, which will be by fire. He warned of the consequences of rejecting God's offer of salvation and living in constant sin (Matthew 25:31-46). When He was confronted by the woman caught in adultery, He said, "Go and sin no more", not continue as you are/were. There is an expectation to turn from sin.

The Apostle Paul wrote about God's wrath being revealed against ALL ungodliness and unrighteousness (Romans 1:18). He also emphasized that believers are saved from God's wrath (not tribulations) through faith in Jesus Christ (Romans 5:9)

God's wrath is not in opposition to His love but rather, it is a facet of His love. God's wrath against sin underscores His love for righteousness and desire to protect and purify His creation. If you love your children, when they constantly refuse to obey you while doing something that may harm them, eventually you turn to wrath to get their attention!

The ultimate expression of God's wrath and love is seen in the crucifixion of Jesus Christ. On the cross, Jesus bore the wrath of God for the sins of humanity, providing a way for people to be reconciled to God if they choose it. The act demonstrates that God's wrath is not vindictive but instead, redemptive, aimed at restoring a broken relationship with His creation. Redemption is a common theme in the Bible.

God's wrath is associated with the final judgement, where those who have rejected God's salvation will face eternal separation from Him (Revelation 20:11-15). This is described as the 'second death' or the Lake of Fire. God is slow to anger, but He does anger. Think of it as a water dam. The dam holds back the water, this is us storing up wrath for ourselves. If we accept Jesus, He takes that wrath instead of us. If we choose to reject Him however, when that dam is broken, those who reject it will feel the full force, poured out, full strength of His wrath for our transgressions and it is a fearful thing to fall into the hands of the living God (Hebrews 10:31). Those unsaved will fall into His hand of judgement. Those people who complain on days the Earth is above 40 degrees will not want to go to Hell. It's much hotter there!!

God's wrath is a response to sin and evil, rooted in His holiness and justice. It serves as a warning and a call to repentance, emphasizing the seriousness of sin and the need for a relationship with God. However, God's wrath is always balanced with His mercy and love, as seen most profoundly in the sacrifice of Jesus Christ, who took on the wrath of God for our redemption. He knew no sin and thus was the only one who qualified to pay that debt for us. You just need to accept that payment. Once you realise the depth of that, your behaviours should change. Do NOT be conformed to this world, but instead be transformed, by the renewing of your mind.

Who is The Anti-Christ Anyway?

The Anti-Christ is a significant figure in end times prophecy, he is described as a charismatic and deceptive leader who will rise to power during the tribulation. He will oppose God and persecute the believers. He is described as 'the man of sin' who exalts himself above all that is called God (2 Thessalonians 2:3-4). One thing we must note is that Jesus says that already, many anti-Christs have come. This suggests that the Anti-Christ is a spirit working through many different people over generations. To eliminate the Jews and the Christians so the Biblical prophecies cannot come to pass. There have been many theories as to who this final man will be.

One thing we do know is that he will appear to have all the answers to the world's problems. He will also usher in peace deals with Israel and the surrounding nations for seven years, also known as the seven prophetic 'weeks' in the book of Daniel. Halfway through this treaty, when everyone is saying peace and security in the Middle East, he will break this treaty, and sudden destruction will come upon them. What follows is anything but peace and safety. At some point he will be badly injured and recover miraculously, he will work many wonders and declare himself as God and expect to be worshipped as God. Revelation 13 portrays the Anti-Christ as the 'beast' who demands worship and enforces the Mark of the Beast system where you will not be able to buy or sell unless you have this mark in the right hand or forehead. Those who resist will be put to death.

Once he enters the Holy place, a great persecution will follow where any Jews in Jerusalem are to head into the mountains. They must not stop to take anything and get out of there immediately. However, the Lord will shorten the days for the sake of the elect.

For anyone paying attention to the world in its current climate, it is not hard to see that the stage has been set for this man to make his appearance in the flesh. I do not know how bad it will need to get before he reveals himself as the world's saviour, but what I do know is he will be Satan in the flesh, just as Jesus was God in the flesh, and is the counterfeit to the real saviour of the world, Jesus Christ.

Pre, Mid or Post Tribulation Rapture?

The word 'rapture' does not appear anywhere in the scripture, but the meaning is to be snatched away suddenly where the real Christians meet the Lord in the air, mentioned in 1 Thessalonians 4:17. In the Bible it does not say that Enoch died. It says that God took him. This is often used as an example of what the rapture will be. When this event does happen, it will be sudden, in the twinkling of an eye, as mentioned in 1 Corinthians 15:52. This is where the saved and unsaved will become most evident. Many people claim to be Christians, yet still endorse what the world says is acceptable. They have a head knowledge of Christ but not a heart knowledge. They have not been born again and display the behaviours in 2 Timothy 3:5:

5 "Having a form of godliness, but denying the power thereof: from such turn away."

These people know the truth but still wish to be part of the world. Do not be one of these people.

As in the days of Noah, so also so the coming of the son of man be. When this event does happen, everyone will be going about their day as normal. Nothing will seem out of the ordinary. Eating, drinking and getting married. We are required to be watchful as we do not know the day or hour the Lord will come and not everyone will be taken during the rapture as Jesus says in Matthew 24:38-42:

"For as in the days that were before the flood they were eating and drinking, marrying and giving in marriage, until the day that Noe entered into the ark,

And knew not until the flood came, and took them all away; so shall also the coming of the Son of man be.

Then shall two be in the field; the one shall be taken, and the other left.

Two women shall be grinding at the mill; the one shall be taken, and the other left.

Watch therefore: for ye know not what hour your Lord doth come." (Matthew 24:38-42)

Let us look at the reasons for and against each of the three beliefs, then I'll go over which one I support and why.

Pre-Tribulation Rapture belief is the rapture will occur before the tribulation, sparing Christians from the period of suffering.

Reasons For:

Imminence: Passages like 1 Thessalonians 4:16-17 and 1 Corinthians 15:51-52 are interpreted to support the idea that the rapture could happen at any moment without preceding events.

God's Wrath: Revelation 3:10 is seen as a promise that believers will be kept from the "hour of trial" that is coming upon the whole world.

Distinction between Church and Israel: Some argue that the tribulation period is primarily for the nation of Israel, not the church, based on Daniel 9:24-27.

Reasons Against:

Lack of Explicit Timing: Critics argue that there is no explicit biblical passage that clearly states the rapture will happen before the tribulation.

Historical Interpretation: Some theologians note that the pre-tribulation rapture theory is a relatively recent development in Christian theology, becoming popular in the 19th century.

Church History: Early church fathers did not explicitly teach a pre-tribulation rapture, suggesting it might not have been the original apostolic teaching.

Mid-Tribulation Rapture belief is the rapture will occur in the middle of the tribulation, after the first half of relative peace and before the great suffering of the second half.

Reasons For:

The Seventh Trumpet: 1 Corinthians 15:52 mentions the "last trumpet," which some interpret as the seventh trumpet in Revelation 11:15, signalling the midpoint of the tribulation.

Two Halves of Tribulation: Daniel 9:27 and Revelation 12:14 describe a division in the tribulation period, suggesting a significant event could occur at the midpoint.

Protection of Believers: Revelation 12:6,14 suggests a period of protection for God's people during part of the tribulation.

Reasons Against:

Ambiguity: The mid-tribulation view relies on interpreting symbolic passages, which can be understood in various ways.

Lack of Clear Evidence: There is no clear biblical statement placing the rapture specifically at the midpoint of the tribulation.

Inconsistency: Some argue that the mid-tribulation view does not align consistently with the doctrine of imminence found in passages like Matthew 24:36.

Post-Tribulation Rapture is the belief the rapture will occur at the end of the tribulation, with believers being caught up to meet Christ as He returns to establish His kingdom on the earth.

Reasons For:

Second Coming: Matthew 24:29-31 describes the return of Christ after the tribulation, at which point believers are gathered to Him.

Single Event: Some passages, such as 2 Thessalonians 2:1-4, suggest that the rapture and the Second Coming of Christ are aspects of a single event rather than two separate events.

Endurance of Believers: Passages like Revelation 13:7 and 14:12 speak of the endurance of the saints through the tribulation, implying their presence during this period.

Reasons Against:

God's Wrath: Critics argue that it is inconsistent with God's character to allow His people to endure the full wrath of the tribulation.

Imminence Undermined: The post-tribulation view may undermine the doctrine of imminence, as it requires specific tribulation events to precede the rapture.

Complexity: The post-tribulation view can be seen as complex, requiring a rapid sequence of events (rapture, Second Coming, and judgement) in a short period.

Arguments can be made for all three, but I subscribe to the post-tribulation rapture for a few key reasons. One is that God has allowed his people to suffer, this is seen all through the scriptures. From being in the wilderness for 40 years to being slaves in Babylon etcetera. Secondly, Jesus Himself says we'll experience it in John 16:33:

³³ "These things I have spoken unto you, that in me ye might have peace. **In the world ye shall have tribulation:** but be of good cheer; I have overcome the world."

The disciples asked Jesus plainly and He responded, in Mark 13:18-37 Jesus tells them what will happen. In verse 24 it even says, **after that tribulation**, read it for yourself. Some will argue that it is for the Jews, but Jesus is telling his disciples. They are the first Christians. The only part which you could deem Jewish-specific is when He tells those in Judaea to flee into the mountains.

Thirdly, tribulation is what the world will do to the believers, wrath is what God will do to the world. They are not the same. We will experience tribulations in the world, as Jesus said we would, but we will not experience God's wrath.

1 Thessalonians 5:9:

⁹ "For God hath **not appointed us to wrath**, but to obtain salvation by our Lord Jesus Christ,"

Tribulation is what the people of the world will do to us. God's wrath is what God ultimately does to the world as punishment. Christians are not appointed under wrath, but tribulations are to be expected. There is a difference between tribulation and wrath. The world will turn on us. If you are expecting a pre-tribulation rapture and it doesn't happen, you are likely to be disappointed, consider yourself unworthy, and even fall away because your expected outcome did not happen.

The point of the book is to prevent you from falling away because you know the plan and are prepared. Therefore, be mentally prepared for a post-tribulation rapture. Be ready for the world to come for you, expect the worst and hope for the best. Your chances of falling away reduce significantly because you know what to expect. I think it is wise to be fully prepared for a post-tribulation rapture. To not be prepared means that if you subscribe to pre-tribulation rapture, you are going to find things unbearable when you have to experience it. We need to hope for the best (pre-tribulation) but fully expect and prepare for the worst.

In 2 Timothy 3:1-7:

1 "This know also, that in the last days perilous times shall come.

For men shall be lovers of their own selves, covetous, boasters, proud, blasphemers, disobedient to parents, unthankful, unholy,

Without natural affection, trucebreakers, false accusers, incontinent, fierce, despisers of those that are good,

Traitors, heady, highminded, lovers of pleasures more than lovers of God;

Having a form of godliness, but denying the power thereof: from such turn away.

For of this sort are they which creep into houses, and lead captive silly women laden with sins, led away with divers lusts,

Ever learning, and never able to come to the knowledge of the truth."

Sound familiar? Sin can literally be ordered to your door or viewed on your phone now. When I see the current state of the world, I think there is no doubt we are living in the end times. Your faith needs to be steadfast as we navigate these times and without compromise as your faith is going to be tested and we must hold the line.

The Great 'Falling Away'

The falling away in the last days, is often referred to as "apostasy". It is a re-occurring theme in biblical prophecy. Part of the reason this book has been written is an attempt to prevent as many falling away as possible and the more you know, the less likely that will happen. There are various reasons for this falling away cited in the Bible.

The reasons are:

Deception by false teachers and prophets, mentioned in Matthew 24:11 and 2 Timothy 4:34. The Bible warns false teachers and prophets will emerge, leading many people astray with doctrines that appeal to their desires rather than the truth. This deception will cause people to abandon their faith. Age of the Earth doctrine will be one such deception, as will be the 'love-is-love-mindset'.

Increase of wickedness and lawlessness. Sin IS lawlessness. The increase of sin and lawlessness will result in the people's love for God and righteous doing growing cold. As societal values drift further from biblical teachings, maintaining a strong faith will become more challenging, see Matthew 24:12.

Persecution and tribulation. Matthew 24:9-10 says we will be delivered up and be killed and be hated by all nations for the name of Jesus. Intense persecution and tribulations can cause believers to falter. When faced with suffering and hardship for their faith, some will choose to abandon their faith to escape the persecution. Most people will bow as this gets more intense, but I would encourage you to remain standing, like Daniel's three friends who refused to bow and worship a false idol.

A strong attachment to worldly pleasures and materialism will draw people away from their faith. The allure of wealth, power, and pleasure can overshadow spiritual commitments. God loves the world, we are instructed not to in - 1 John 2:15-17.

A lack of genuine faith! Some people profess faith without a deep and genuine commitment to God. When the trials and temptations come, their superficial faith may not withstand the pressure, leading to apostasy. See 2 Thessalonians 2:3.

The rise of the Anti-Christ and his influence through deception and false miracles will mislead many. Those who do not have a strong love for the truth will be vulnerable during this time. See 2 Thessalonians 2:9-12.

Spiritual warfare, the spiritual battle against evil forces can lead to a weakening of faith. Believers are called to be vigilant, put on the full armour of God and stand firm in Ephesians 6:12.

The secularisation and relativism. The increasing secularisation of society and the rise of moral relativism are eroding traditional religious values. As absolute truths are questioned and moral standards become more subjective, maintaining a firm faith becomes more challenging.

The falling away in the last days is attributed to a combination of deception, persecution, increasing wickedness, love for worldly things, lack of genuine faith, the influence of the Anti-Christ, and ongoing spiritual warfare. These factors highlight the importance of staying rooted in biblical truth, being vigilant, and maintaining a strong, personal relationship with God. As believers we MUST remain steadfast, aware of the coming challenges and be PREPARED to endure to the end. Let's make sure our lamps are full of oil and not be caught off-guard.

The Second Coming of Christ

The Second Coming of Christ is the pivotal moment of end times prophecy. This is where Jesus returns to the earth in power and glory to establish His kingdom. This will be evident by His visible return, seen by all as mentioned in Revelation 1:7. He will then go on to defeat the Anti-Christ and his forces (Revelation 19:11-21). Christ will then establish His millennial reign on the earth

(Revelation 20:4-6). Jesus has told us in advance of the many signs we can watch out for just before His return. We need to be able to recognise the signs of the times and focus on eternity.

Throughout the scripture, it refers to the Day of The Lord. This is the final day of human history where we find out our eternal destiny. The language of Hell is strong in the Bible, for good reason. God does not want you to go there. Going there, however, will be completely your choice. Jesus depicts it as somewhere horrific where He refers to weeping and gnashing of teeth. The unrepentant will reap what they have sown, for God will not be mocked. The Mount of Olives referred to in Zechariah 14:4 is talking about the Second Coming and where Jesus will land. Fun fact, the sermon on the Mount was on the Mount of Olives. How do we know when we are close? Jesus likens these events to a woman in labour, or birth pains, increasing in both frequency and intensity until He arrives giving new life:

Increase in deception. We can see this with the rise of AI and technology. You can lie and deceive more easily than at any point in history. I watched a video produced by AI and you could not tell that it wasn't real! Satan, the father of lies, is really excited about this technology and will use it for his own gain.

Demonic and false teachers, paving the way for the Anti-Christ. Jesus stresses not to be led astray. For many will come in my name, people claiming to be a Christian or saying, "I'm a good person," etcetera. Some even saying they are the Christ. This is why you need to know the Bible for yourself so you will not be deceived.

Wars and rumours of wars. Many people will tell you that there have always been wars and rumours of wars. The difference today is that they are all happening at the same time and nation is rising against nation. This is what makes it distinct. We can see it all in real-time instantly, with many nations rising up and fighting each other. There has been an increase in wars over the last 30 years. As I'm writing this book, both Turkey and Iran have threatened to invade Israel, these two nations are predicted to attack Israel in the end times as the war of Gog and Magog. With these two nations being the modern-day countries to attack Israel, they just need Russia to complete the prophecy.

Increase in natural disasters, such as earthquakes, famines, and plagues, in various places.

The real Christians will be hated. Matthew 24:9 describes being delivered up to tribulation and being killed. This is another reason I do not believe a pre-tribulation rapture. We are now in a world where the Bible is considered immoral. Social 'justice' is sin, re-applied by evil, pride-filled people. There will be increasing persecution for those people of God.

People will fall away and betray each other and hate one another (Matthew 24:10). Otherwise called apostasy. One of the reasons this book has been written is because I've seen it firsthand with many accommodating the world and its teachings. This is a complete lack of courage.

Increase in lawlessness. Sin is lawlessness and the violation of God's commandments. This increase in evil will cause the love of many people to grow cold.

Global evangelism. This is being done via the internet and people out there doing it through mission work. If you are hearing the gospel, there is still hope from them. Because God is Holy, He cannot take us as we are, that's why we needed a saviour in the first place. People will not be able to say they didn't know the news of the gospel, and then shall the end come. Until that last time, there is still time to repent, but at some point, that grace will end.

The Millennial Kingdom

The Millennial Kingdom is the period described where Christ has a reign of 1000 years on the earth. Jesus bounds Satan and imprisons him for this 1000-year period. During the 1000 years, the earth will experience a time of peace, righteousness and justice. The believers who have been martyred for their faith in Christ will be resurrected to reign with Christ (Revelation 20:4-6).

After these 1000 years, Satan will be released from prison to again deceive the nations. After 1000 years of peace, humanity will again fall for his deception demonstrating how fickle the human heart can be, even after 1000 years of peace!

The Final Judgement

The Final Judgement, also known as the Great White Throne Judgement, occurs after the Millennial Kingdom. It is the ultimate judgement of all of humanity, both living and dead, where each person's eternal destiny is determined based on their relationship with Christ. The final judgement is universal, meaning that all people will be judged regardless of their status, wealth or position. The most crucial criterion for judgement is whether a person has placed their faith in Jesus Christ as Lord AND Saviour. Those who have accepted Christ and followed Him will be granted eternal life (John 3:16 and Ephesians 2:8-9). While salvation is by faith, the Bible teaches that deeds and actions are evidence of that faith (James 2:14-26). Believers will be rewarded based on their faithfulness, and those who have rejected God will be judged according to their works. Revelation 20:12-15 mentions the Book of Life, in which the names of those who have received eternal life are written. Those names in this book are saved, while those not found will face eternal punishment.

For believers, the Final Judgement is a source of hope, as it promises the ultimate vindication and the fulfilment of God's promises. Faithfulness is rewarded while also affirming that evil and sin will be dealt with fully and fairly, and every wrong made right.

The scene of the final judgement in Revelation 20:11-15, describes the dead being judged according to their works and those not found in the Book of Life, are cast into the Lake of Fire. We do not want to be in that lake!

The New Heaven and New Earth

Once the final judgement is completed, God will create a new heaven and a new earth, this is the place where the righteous will dwell, the earth as it was originally meant to be before the fall, fully restored. This is what every Christian, and even every person is praying and hoping for. Even unbelievers want this peace. It is amazing to me that many will not choose it.

Here the holy city of New Jerusalem will descend from heaven, where God Himself will dwell with His people where there will be no more death, sorrow or pain, and the believers will enjoy eternal fellowship with God, our creator.

1 Corinthians 15:26:

[26] "**The last enemy** that shall be destroyed **is death.**"

This hope of final redemption is the hope that is within you and is what we seek. Know that with all these trials and tribulations, that peace comes to pass at the end. Be hopeful and do not fear the things of the world. This is God's ultimate plan for humanity. I cannot emphasize enough the importance of faith, readiness and hope that is for the believers in Christ. For without faith, it is impossible to please Him. Hebrews 11:6:

[6] "**But without faith it is impossible to please him: for he that cometh to God must believe that he is, and that he is a rewarder of them that diligently seek him.**"

Knowing it for Yourself

Knowing the Bible for yourself is crucial for several reasons, especially in the context of personal faith, spiritual growth, and understanding of God's will. Here are some key reasons why it's important for you to personally engage with the Bible and not just rely on an hour in church every week.

Direct Connection: The Bible is God's Word, revealing His character, promises, and plans. By reading and studying the Bible personally, you develop a direct relationship with God, allowing Him to speak to you through scripture.

Spiritual Growth: Personal engagement with the Bible deepens your understanding of God's nature, helps you grow in faith, and strengthens your spiritual life. It allows you to cultivate a deeper, more intimate relationship with God.

Discernment: In a world filled with various beliefs and interpretations, knowing the Word for yourself helps you discern truth from falsehood. This is why so many will fall away because they do not do this! It equips you to evaluate teachings, sermons and advice against the Word of God, ensuring you are not led astray.

Sound Doctrine: Personal study ensures that your beliefs are based on scripture rather than human opinions or traditions. It helps you build a strong foundation of sound doctrine, rooted in the truth of God's Word.

Life Guide: The Bible offers wisdom and guidance for every aspect of life, including relationships, decision-making, and moral choices. When you know the Bible for yourself, you can apply its teachings directly to your life, making informed godly decisions.

Transformation: As you read, listen, and meditate on God's Word, it shapes your character, renews your mind, and helps you conform more closely to the image of Christ.

Informed Prayer: Knowing scripture enriches your prayer life. You can pray more effectively and confidently when you are familiar with God's promises and the Biblical truths.

Authentic Worship: This allows you to worship God with a clearer understanding of who He is and what He has done. We are all made to worship something, some worship football teams, and some worship sex.

Sharing the Gospel: Knowing the Bible equips you to share your faith with others and allows you to accurately communicate the message of the gospel and answer questions or challenges with confidence and boldness.

Independent Study: While teachers, pastors, and mentors are valuable, personal Bible study ensures that your faith is not solely dependent on others' interpretations or teachings. The scripture isn't open to any private interpretation (2 Peter 1:20).

Avoiding Misinterpretation: Knowing it for yourself reduces the risk of being misled by inaccurate or distorted teachings, and helps you spot inconsistencies or errors in others' interpretations.

Biblical Mandate: The Bible itself encourages believers to know and meditate on scripture. In Psalm 1:2, it speaks of the blessedness of those who delight in and meditate on God's law, day and night. In Joshua 1:8, it similarly emphasizes the importance of meditation on the law and obeying it.

Knowing the Bible for yourself is essential for developing a deep, personal relationship with God, discerning truth, applying God's Word to your life, and effectively living out your faith. It empowers you to grow spiritually, resist temptation, endure trials, and share the gospel with confidence. One of the godliest men in the Bible, Daniel was exiled and held in Babylon long before we had printed Bibles.

In Daniel 9:2:

² "In the first year of his reign **I Daniel understood by books the number of the years, whereof the word of the Lord came to Jeremiah the prophet, that he would accomplish seventy years in the desolations of Jerusalem."**

Daniel was a godly man and just by studying the writings of the prophet Jeremiah, he understood that the 70 years of exile were nearly completed! But the rest of the people did not and were not ready to leave Babylon! Daniel, who was exiled as a young man, possibly a teenager, and through the sins of previous generations still accepted responsibility and prayed for the people. I encourage you to pray for those who do not perceive the signs of the times and that they study for themselves.

Conclusion

The teachings on the end times have profound and practical implications for believers. They call for a life of spiritual preparedness, imbued with hope and encouragement, driven with a sense of urgency in evangelism and mission, and characterised by ethical and holy living. The more knowledge we have about end times events, the more confident we should be in the scriptures. Knowing the plan will prevent us from falling away because we can recognise the signs of the times. This does not mean that it will be easy, but we must be focused on eternity.

We need to know who God is. There is coming a day when His grace and patience will expire and the Day of the Lord, our final day, will be upon us. Joel 2:11-12:

¹¹ "And the Lord shall utter his voice before his army: for his camp is very great: for he is strong that executeth his word: for the Day of the Lord is great and very terrible; and who can abide it?

¹² Therefore also now, saith the Lord, turn **ye even to me with all your heart**, and with fasting, and with weeping, and with mourning"

In verse 12, He is calling for us to return to Him **ALL** our heart. Most people do not give Him all of it. Maybe there are some sins you enjoy and are holding on to. Nobody who has given God 100% of their heart has regretted it. How much of your heart does God have? Be honest with yourself. God wants your whole heart. It is what is best for you. Is your relationship with God your **highest** priority? Are we leading our children in who the Lord is and how to pray? Our, world has become so dark, and if we do not lead our children and all they experience is the world as it is, how can they experience life and joy? What is your behaviour saying about your faith in your God? If you claim to be Christian yet do not repent, God cannot bless you.

Trusting God can be hard at times, especially what we see around us in the world. However, God has shown us in advance what to expect as time moves forward. As children, we often did not know why our parents told us to do and not do certain actions. For the most part, we trusted their judgement until we got old enough to rebel! God exists in eternity; His ways are higher than our ways and thoughts higher than ours. We can trust Him to see us through just as He did for Job and Joseph.

If we repent and put 100% of our trust and faith in Him, it heals our relationship with God and ultimately filters down to every relationship in our life. The Bible says that EVERY knee shall bow, and EVERY tongue shall confess Jesus is Lord, those who haven't accepted His salvation will bow at His glory but will not go into heaven.

In Revelation 3:20, we read that God stands at the door and knocks, if any man hears and opens the door, He will come in. This is inviting the Holy Spirit to dwell within you. Take Him seriously because He will not knock forever. At some point, He will give you over to your desires. If you hear that knocking and/or His voice at the door, I encourage you to open the door! You won't regret doing so.

www.ingramcontent.com/pod-product-compliance
Lightning Source LLC
Chambersburg PA
CBHW052015070526
44584CB00016B/1763